Cordon Bleu

Summer
Cookery

Cordon Bleu

Summer Cookery

CBC/B.P.C. Publishing Ltd.

Published by
B.P.C. Publishing Ltd.,
P.O. Box 20,
Abingdon, Oxon.

Designed by Melvyn Kyte
Printed and bound in England
by Waterlow (Dunstable) Limited

These recipes have been adapted from the Cordon Bleu Cookery Course
published by Purnell in association with the London Cordon Bleu Cookery
School
Principal: Rosemary Hume; Co-Principal: Muriel Downes

Quantities given are for 4 servings unless more are specified.
Spoon measures are level unless otherwise stated.

Contents

Introduction

Cooking in the summer can be just plain hard work — or it can be tremendous fun. A Cordon Bleu cook will plan to make it a pleasure for herself, the family and guests. All you have to do is to pick the dishes that suit the weather and the occasion.

Summer is the ideal time for informal meals, so make light work of parties and socials. Eating in the open adds romance whether you are in the garden or farther afield. To make the best of this you may cook in advance and carry a packed meal with you. Or, if you have the equipment, you can cook on the spot and everybody can lend a hand. We hope our brief survey of barbecue equipment will help you here.

A cold table, carefully prepared, will help any party go with a swing, and a mixture of old favourites and a few imaginative surprises will make your open air menus a delight to all your friends. Choose this method of entertaining if the food is not intended as the focal point of your gathering, for then your guests can 'cut and come again' at will.

Formal entertaining doesn't stop just because the sun has come out. Here the greatest skill is required in choosing food that is light enough to be enjoyed in hot weather without being monotonous. Our planned 3-course meals at the beginning of this book are designed to help you with just this choice. We have carefully mixed hot and cold foods, and there are many dishes that can be prepared in advance. To take the worry out of entertaining we have given you timetables which show just when to prepare each course so that you are ready on time without any last minute fluster.

Don't neglect your summer thirst when preparing these delicious meals. Our section on ices and drinks is designed to refresh the most discerning palate. Adults and children will love you if you take the time to make your own fruit drinks and ices.

In our appendix, we have also included a glossary of some of the special cooking terms used and notes on the preparation of various items that recur throughout the book. Experienced cooks may not need to use this, but if there is anything you do not

7

understand in a recipe you will
probably find it further explained
in the appendix.

Rosemary Hume
Muriel Downes

You will find that **cooking times** given in individual recipes in this book have sometimes been adapted in the timetables to help you when cooking and serving the menus as three-course meals.

3~course summer meals

Tempt your summer guests with meals that appeal to hot-weather appetites. Offer a mixture of hot and cold dishes, and contrasting textures. Crisp with creamy, sweet with sharp — these are the combinations that will please.
And so that you can be a cool and collected host or hostess, follow our timetables for preparation and cooking. You'll be surprised how much easier it is to entertain if you don't leave all the work till the last minute — and what compliments there'll be afterwards !

Menu 1 Fish

Starter : Asparagus with melted butter

Main course : Stuffed trout Nantua with new potatoes

Dessert : Strawberry tabatières

TIMETABLE

Day before
Poach trout.
Prepare prawn mousse.
Make mayonnaise.
Make praline, crush and
store in airtight container.

Morning
Prepare asparagus and tie
in bundles for boiling.
Scrape potatoes.
Skin and bone trout and
fill with mousse.
Make and bake choux
pastry. Make pastry cream.
Hull strawberries and
brush with glaze.
Wash watercress and cut
cucumber; chop parsley.
Assemble ingredients ready
for final cooking from 7.00
for dinner around 8 pm.

Order of work

7.00 Whip cream, add
praline and fill
tabatières; arrange on
serving dish.

7.15 Add paprika and Tabasco
sauce (or tomato juice)
to mayonnaise ;
dish up trout and
garnish with cucumber.

7.30 Put asparagus and
potatoes to cook.

7.45 Drain asparagus, dish up
and keep warm. Melt butter.
Drain potatoes, dry and
leave in pan with
folded napkin on top to
absorb the steam ;
keep them warm.

8.00 Serve first course.
Drop butter and parsley
into saucepan of
potatoes when ready
to serve.

Asparagus with melted butter

1-2 bundles of asparagus
4 oz butter

Method

Trim the bottom stalks of the asparagus, leaving about 2-3 inches before the green starts. To make sure that all stalks are the same length, cut them while asparagus is still tied in bundles. After untying them, rinse stalks well in cold water and then, using a small vegetable knife, scrape the white part of the stems well and stand them in a bowl of cold water. Now tie the spears together in bundles, according to size, with fine string ; leave the cut stems standing in cold water until you are ready to cook them.

Have ready a deep pan of plenty of boiling salted water and stand the asparagus spears in this, stalk end down ; cook gently, covered, for 12-15 minutes or until the green part is tender.

Watchpoint The green tips should stand above the water and cook just in the steam.

Lift spears carefully from the pan, drain them well on clean muslin and then place them on a folded napkin in a hot serving dish. Cut and remove the string from each bundle. Melt the butter gently in a small pan, but do not let it get too hot and oily. Then skim it well and pour into a hot sauce boat and serve separately.

Stuffed trout Nantua

4-5 even-size trout
court bouillon (for poaching) — see page 133
½ pint mayonnaise (see page 137)
pinch of paprika pepper
¼ teaspoon Tabasco sauce, or 1-2 tablespoons tomato juice cocktail

For prawn mousse
8 oz prawns (shelled)
¼ pint thick béchamel sauce (see page 138)
2 oz butter (creamed)
salt and pepper
2 tablespoons double cream (partially whipped)

For garnish
½ cucumber and sprigs of watercress, or extra prawns

Method

Poach the trout in court bouillon and leave to cool. Remove skin and bones.

To prepare prawn mousse : mince prawns and pound them with the cold béchamel sauce, or work together in a blender. Add the creamed butter, adjust the seasoning and fold in the cream.

Stuff each trout with the prawn mixture and arrange on a serving dish. Season the mayonnaise with paprika and Tabasco sauce (or tomato juice cocktail) and spoon a little over each trout ; hand the remainder separately.

For garnish : slice or dice the cucumber, sprinkle with salt and press between two plates. Drain off any liquid after 30 minutes, then arrange cucumber around dish with watercress (or prawns).

Serve with new potatoes, boiled, buttered and sprinkled with chopped parsley.

11

Strawberry tabatières

½ lb strawberries (hulled)
6 tablespoons redcurrant glaze (see page 133)
¼ pint double cream

For choux pastry
3 oz butter
7½ fl oz water
3¾ oz plain flour (sifted)
3 eggs

For pastry cream
1 egg (separated)
1 egg yolk
2 oz caster sugar
2-3 drops of vanilla essence
1 rounded tablespoon plain flour
1 tablespoon cornflour
½ pint milk

For praline
2 oz almonds (unblanched)
2 oz caster sugar

Method

Set oven at 400°F or Mark 6.

First make choux pastry : boil butter and water together, draw pan aside, allow bubbles to subside, then shoot in all the flour at once. Stir the mixture vigorously until it is smooth. Cool it slightly, then beat in the eggs thoroughly, one at a time. The dough should then be smooth and glossy. Pipe out the choux on to a dampened baking sheet in the shape of small turnovers and bake in pre-set oven for about 20 minutes until crisp to the touch.

To prepare pastry cream : cream the egg yolks, sugar and vanilla essence together until the mixture looks white ; add the flours and a little cold milk and make into a smooth paste. Heat the remaining milk and pour it on to the egg mixture, blend together and return to pan. Stir cream over the heat until boiling, then draw pan aside. Stiffly whip the egg white.

Turn one-third of the pastry cream into a bowl, fold in the egg white gradually, then return mixture to the pan containing the remaining cream and stir gently over heat for 2-3 minutes to set the egg white. Turn cream into a bowl, cover and leave to cool.

To make praline : put almonds and sugar into a small, heavy pan ; cook over a low heat and stir with a metal spoon when the sugar begins to colour. Continue stirring while the sugar dissolves and turns a good deep brown. The praline is ready when the nuts are well toasted (beginning to crackle). Turn praline on to an oiled baking sheet and leave to cool ; then crush with a rolling pin, or use a nut mill or cheese grater.

Lightly whip the double cream and fold it into the pastry cream, adding enough praline to flavour it well. Split the cold choux pastry and fill with the praline cream. Arrange the strawberries, dipped in or brushed with warm redcurrant glaze, round the edge of each 'tabatière'. Then arrange on serving dish.

> **Tabatière** is the French word for a snuff-box, snuff being 'tabac (tobacco) à prise'. This recipe is so called because the choux pastry is folded into a turn-over shape, similar to that of a tobacco pouch.

Menu 2 Beef

Starter : Eggs Connaught

Main course : Médaillons de bœuf with potato vinaigrette and French beans

Dessert : Apricot moscovite with pains de seigle

TIMETABLE

Day before
Roast fillet of beef.
If using home-made aspic, prepare it.
Make pains de seigle and store in airtight container.
Cook apricots and prepare custard for moscovite but do not add gelatine yet ; cover and keep both in a cool place.

Morning
Hardboil eggs and prepare filling. Keep filling covered in small bowl and egg whites in a bowl of cold water.
Finish apricot moscovite and sauce.
Make up powdered aspic, if using.
Cut beef and ham, spread creamed pâté on beef rounds and cover with ham.
Coat with aspic.
Cook potatoes and beans.
Prepare dressings.
Assemble equipment for final cooking from 6.30 for dinner around 8 pm.

Order of work

6.30 Fill eggs and dish up. Cut brown bread and butter.

6.45 Toss potatoes and beans in dressing.

7.00 Turn out and decorate moscovite and put aside with sauce until ready to serve.

8.00 Serve first course.

Eggs Connaught

6 hard-boiled eggs
$\frac{1}{4}$ pint milk
1 slice of onion
blade of mace
6 peppercorns
$3\frac{1}{2}$ oz butter
1 tablespoon plain flour
salt and pepper
1 packet Demi-Sel cheese
1 teaspoon paprika pepper
4 oz prawns (shelled)
$\frac{1}{2}$ bunch of watercress (to garnish)

Method

Scald the milk with the onion, mace and peppercorns, tip into a jug, cover and leave to infuse. Rinse the pan with cold water, drop in $\frac{1}{2}$ oz butter, heat gently and blend in the flour. Strain on the milk and add salt. Stir continuously, bring milk to the boil, cook 1 minute. Turn on to a plate, cover with buttered paper to prevent a skin forming and leave sauce until cold. Cream remaining butter until soft.

Split the hard-boiled eggs in two, scoop out the yolks and rub through a wire strainer; keep the whites in a bowl of water as they soon get hard if exposed to air. Work the yolks with the butter, cheese, paprika and cold sauce. Chop half the prawns finely, add to the mixture

While rubbing yolks through a strainer, keep whites in cold water

and season to taste. Drain and dry the egg whites and have ready a round serving dish or use a cake platter.

Spoon a drop of filling on to the dish to hold each egg white in position, arrange them in a circle and then fill each with the mixture, or you can use a piping bag with a $\frac{1}{2}$-inch plain pipe. Scatter over the remaining prawns (split in half, if large) and dust with paprika. Place the watercress in the middle and serve brown bread and butter separately.

For a very special party this recipe can be prepared with smoked salmon in place of prawns. Save a little smoked salmon to cut into fine shreds and scatter over.

The stuffed eggs are scattered with prawns and garnished with cress

To hardboil eggs

Cooked in the following way, the yolks will be set in the middle of the whites and have no dark rings round them. Have a saucepan of boiling water, draw to one side and put in the eggs which should be at room temperature. (Eggs taken from a refrigerator and plunged into fast-boiling water will crack.) After the water has reboiled, cook 9 minutes for small eggs, 10 for large. Tip off the hot water and cool quickly under a running tap.

Médaillons de bœuf

1 lb fillet of beef (in the piece)
2-3 tablespoons dripping, or oil
8 oz pâté de foie
2-3 oz butter (creamed)
1 truffle, or 6-8 button mushrooms
$\frac{1}{4}$ teaspoon Dijon mustard (optional)
1-2 teaspoons sherry (optional)
8 oz ham, or cooked gammon
    (sliced)
1$\frac{1}{2}$ pints aspic jelly (see page 132)

Below : spreading slices of beef with pâté de foie mixed with butter
Bottom : having set the beef and ham slices in aspic, garnish with truffle and cover with more aspic

Method

Set the oven at 400°F or Mark 7. Tie the fillet into a good shape. Heat 2-3 tablespoons dripping, or oil, in a tin and when hot put in the fillet. Baste, turn and baste again. Lift joint on to a wire rack and place rack in roasting tin. Roast for 30-35 minutes, basting twice and turning the meat half way through cooking time. Leave until quite cold. Work the pâté de foie with the butter and, if you are using truffle to garnish, add the trimmings (finely chopped) to flavour ; if not, add the Dijon mustard and sherry.

Cut the fillet in $\frac{1}{4}$-inch thick slices ; trim and cut a round of ham to fit each slice of beef. Pipe or carefully spread a layer of pâté on top of each piece of fillet and lay the slices of ham on top. Press lightly together and smooth round the edge. Lay these pieces (they should be about $\frac{1}{2}$ inch thick) in a shallow dish or tin and spoon in just enough cold, but still liquid, aspic to cover. Leave until just set, then garnish each piece with a slice of truffle or a whole cooked mushroom. (Wipe button mushrooms and cook in a little water and lemon juice for 1-2 minutes. Do not use butter or oil which would cloud the aspic.) Coat again with cold aspic and leave until set.

To serve : cut round the slices in aspic with a round or oval cutter and dish up, surrounding with the remaining aspic (chopped). Serve with boiled new potatoes dressed with vinaigrette and cooked French beans tossed in French dressing (salad dressings are on page 137).

Apricot moscovite

½ lb apricots (poached until tender in a syrup made from ½ pint water and 3 oz granulated sugar — see page 136) — soak dried apricots overnight before poaching
½ pint milk
3 egg yolks
3 oz caster sugar
scant ½ oz gelatine
¼ pint double cream (lightly whipped)
3-4 tablespoons brandy (optional)

For decoration (optional)
extra double cream (whipped)
crushed praline (see page 12)

Jelly mould (1-1½ pint capacity)

Method
Scald milk, cream the egg yolks with the sugar, pour on the scalded milk, blend and then return custard to pan. Thicken over heat without boiling, strain and cool.

Drain the apricots, reserving the syrup, and rub them through a nylon strainer. Divide this purée into two and put one half in the refrigerator to chill.

Dissolve the gelatine over gentle heat in $2\frac{1}{2}$ fl oz of the apricot syrup and add it to the egg custard. Add the chilled apricot purée to the cream. When the custard is on the point of setting, fold in the apricot cream, flavour with 1-2 tablespoons brandy, and turn into the oiled mould to set.

Flavour the remaining purée with the rest of the brandy to make an apricot sauce and add the reserved syrup. Turn out the mould on to a serving dish, decorate with a little extra cream and praline, and pour round the sauce. Serve with pains de seigle.

Pains de seigle

4 oz ground almonds
4 oz caster sugar
scant 1 oz plain flour
2 egg whites (lightly beaten)
2 oz praline (pounded and sieved — see page 12)
icing sugar

Rice paper

This recipe makes about 24 petits fours.

Method
Set the oven at 350°F or Mark 4. Mix the almonds, sugar and flour together and pass them through a wire sieve. Moisten with about three-quarters of the egg whites, adding this gradually and pounding well. Work in the praline.

Divide the mixture into small pieces, each the size of a walnut, roll them first in the remaining egg white and then in a little icing sugar. Bake on rice paper on a baking sheet in the pre-set oven for about 15 minutes. Cool them on a wire rack and store in an airtight tin until wanted.

Piping the whipped cream on to the apricot mould after turning it out

Menu 3 Beef and pigeon

Starter : Cod's roe pâté

Main course : Cold beefsteak, pigeon and mushroom pie
with potato mayonnaise

Dessert : Coupe française

TIMETABLE

Day before
Make pastry for pie.
Cook pigeons and beef.
Make mayonnaise and
French dressing. Scrub and
cook potatoes, peel them,
slice, if necessary, and coat
with French dressing, leave
uncovered in a bowl in the
larder or a cool place.
Prepare mushrooms for pie.
Bake pie and add extra aspic
to it if necessary when the
pie is cooked but still warm.

Morning
Make coupe, cover each
glass with foil and keep
in refrigerator.
Make cod's roe pâté and put
on serving dish.
Quarter lemons ; put them
and olives into separate
dishes. Put the butter into a
dish, and cut bread ready
for making toast and keep
in a polythene bag.
Assemble ingredients for
final preparation from 7.30 for
dinner around 8 pm.

Order of work

7.30 Remove foil from coupes
and pile strawberries
or cherries on top.
Mix mayonnaise with
potato and arrange on
serving dish with
garnish.

7.50 Make toast for serving
pâté.

8.00 Serve first course.

Cod's roe pâté

12 oz smoked cod's roe (in the
  piece), or an 8 oz jar
1 teaspoon onion juice (from grated
  onion)
¼ pint olive oil
1 cup fresh white breadcrumbs, or
  3-4 slices of bread
1 packet Demi-Sel cheese
lemon, or tomato, juice (to taste)
pepper

To garnish
toast (hot, dry)
unsalted butter
black olives
lemon quarters

Method

Scrape the roe from the skin and
put in a bowl with the onion
juice. Pour the oil over the
breadcrumbs and leave to soak
for 5 minutes (if using slices of
bread, remove the crust, put
bread in a dish and sprinkle with
the oil). Pound or beat the cod's
roe with the Demi-Sel cheese
until quite smooth, then work in
the breadcrumbs and oil, a
little at a time. Finish with lemon
(or tomato) juice to taste and
season with pepper. The mixture
should be light and creamy.

Pile into a shallow dish and
serve with hot, dry toast (served
between the folds of a napkin),
unsalted butter, black olives and
quarters of lemon in separate
dishes.

1 *Scraping a piece of smoked cod's
roe from the skin into a mortar*
2 *Pounding together the roe and the
Demi-Sel cheese, while breadcrumbs
soak in oil*
3 *Dishing up the pâté ready to serve
with toast, black olives and lemon*

Beefsteak, pigeon and mushroom pie

1½ lb shin of beef (cut into 1-inch
  squares)
2 pigeons
1 oz butter
2 pints chicken stock (see page 139)
salt and pepper
½ pint aspic jelly (commercially
  prepared)
¼ lb flat mushrooms
8 oz quantity of flaky, or puff,
  pastry (see page 135)
1 egg (beaten)
pinch of salt

9-inch long pie dish

Method
Melt the butter in a large stew-pan, add the pigeons and brown slowly. Remove from the dish, split in half and return to the dish with the squares of beef and the stock. Season with salt and pepper, cover and cook slowly on top of the stove for 2-2½ hours. Then cut the breast meat from the pigeons and discard the carcass; add the aspic to the pan, turn out into a bowl and leave to get cold. Set the oven at 425°F or Mark 7.

Wash and trim the mushrooms, cut in quarters and put in a pie dish with the cooked meats and liquid. Place a pie funnel in the middle of the dish. Roll out the pastry to an oblong just under ¼ inch thick and about 3 inches wider and 4 inches longer than your pie dish. Cut off extra pastry; roll these trimmings to ⅛ inch thick. From this thinner pastry, cut strips to fit on the rim of the pie dish, and make leaves and a thistle, or rose, from the pastry, for decoration. Dampen the rim of the pie dish and cover with a strip of pastry, pressing it firmly in position, then brush the pastry with cold water. Lift the thicker piece of pastry on your rolling pin and lay it carefully over the top of the pie, taking care not to stretch it. Trim it and press the two layers of pastry on the rim very firmly together; seal and flute the edges.

Add a large pinch of salt to the beaten egg and beat lightly with a fork until the salt dissolves and the egg darkens in colour, this will give the pastry a rich brown and shiny glaze. Brush the top of the pie with the prepared egg wash, decorate suitably with pastry leaves, make a hole in the pastry in the centre of the leaves (above pie funnel) to allow for the escape of steam during cooking time. Brush the decoration with egg wash. Cook the rose or thistle on a baking sheet and put on pie when cooked.

Bake in pre-set oven for about 20-25 minutes, until pastry is cooked. While the pie is still warm add a little more liquid aspic through hole in centre, if necessary. Serve cold, with potato mayonnaise.

Adding cooked pigeon breasts and beef to quartered mushrooms

22

Potato mayonnaise

1-1½ lb new potatoes
3-4 tablespoons French dressing
    (see page 137)
salt and pepper
¼ pint thick mayonnaise (see page
    137)

To garnish
6 pickled walnuts
paprika pepper (optional)

Method

Scrub the potatoes and cook in their skins in boiling salted water until tender. Drain and dry, peel while still hot and cut in thick slices if the potatoes are large but keep whole if really small. Put in a bowl and moisten at once with the French dressing ; season, cover and leave until cold.

When ready to serve, take 2 tablespoons of the mayonnaise, mix in carefully and turn potatoes into a dish. Thin the remaining mayonnaise with 1 dessertspoon of boiling water and spoon over the salad. Slice the pickled walnuts and arrange around the dish. Sprinkle the top with paprika, if liked.

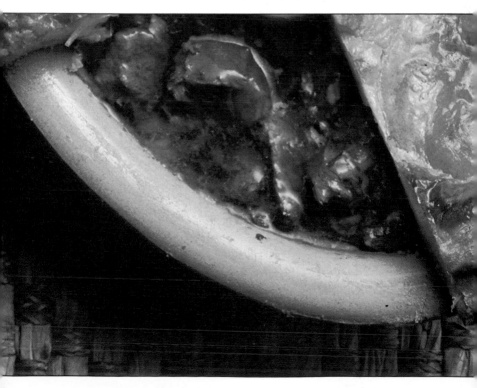

Coupe française

¼ pint milk
thinly pared rind of ½ lemon
2 egg yolks
1 oz caster sugar
1 teaspoon gelatine (soaked in
  2 tablespoons water)
½ teaspoon vanilla essence
1 small carton (2½ fl oz) double
  cream
1 egg white

To finish
about 20 fresh strawberries with
  1 tablespoon caster sugar,
  or bright red canned cherries

4-5 coupe glasses

Method
Infuse the milk with the lemon rind. Cream the egg yolks and sugar together until thick and light in colour. Tip the hot milk on to the yolks then strain back into the saucepan. Stir the mixture over gentle heat until the custard coats the back of the wooden spoon, then add the soaked gelatine and stir until melted.

Watchpoint Do not allow to boil. To cut down the risk of overheating and consequent curdling, a double saucepan may be used to thicken the custard.

Cool the mixture, then add the vanilla essence and cream. Whisk the egg white until stiff, fold into the creamy mixture and stir gently (standing the bowl in a second one containing ice cubes and water) until the mixture begins to thicken. Pour quickly into the coupe glasses and leave until set.

Arrange the strawberries (sprinkled with sugar), or the drained cherries, in a pyramid on top of each coupe.

Serve as cold as possible.

Menu 4 Chicken

Starter : Tomatoes Gervais

Main course : Chicken Véronique with julienne potato cake and
green salad

Dessert : Chocolate mousse basque with cigarettes russes

TIMETABLE

Day before
Make chocolate mousses
and cigarettes russes.

Morning
Make chicken stock. Peel
potatoes, leave whole in
water. Prepare salad, wrap
in absorbent paper then in
tea-towel, put in bowl in
refrigerator.
Season, put butter inside
trussed chicken ; set
chicken in roasting tin,
cover with buttered paper,
keep in larder until ready
for cooking.
Make French dressing, scald
tomatoes, put immediately
in cold water, drain but do
not skin yet.
Prepare cream cheese
mixture, cover with foil or
greaseproof paper.
Peel and pip grapes, keep
in refrigerator.
Assemble equipment for
final cooking from 5.45
for dinner around 8 pm.

Order of work
5.45 Light oven.
Dry and cut potatoes ;
butter pan, fill with
potato strips.
Put chicken in oven.
Whip cream and

decorate chocolate
mousses. Skin and fill
tomatoes, dish up and
put to chill.
Baste chicken, turn on
side. Baste, turn chicken
on to other side
5 minutes later.
Wrap brown loaf,
refrigerate for
30 minutes.

7.00 Cut bread and butter.
Put potatoes to cook,
baste chicken, turn
breast side up.
Take up chicken, turn
oven to low ; make
gravy but do not add
grapes or cream yet.
Carve chicken, put back
in roasting tin with
gravy. Lay greaseproof
paper on top but do not
tie or fix over edge.
Return to bottom of
oven.
Potatoes, if nicely
coloured, can now be
put on top shelf of the
oven to finish cooking.
Toss green salad.

8.00 Turn out potatoes,
arrange chicken on top.
Cover with foil, keep
hot. Add cream and
grapes to gravy, keep
hot.
Serve first course.

Tomatoes Gervais

8 tomatoes
salt and pepper
4 oz cream cheese (2 packets
  Gervais, or loose curd cheese,
  or home-made)
small bunch of fresh chives (or
  chopped parsley, or spring onion
  tops, or snipped watercress stalks)
2-3 tablespoons double cream,
  or top of milk
watercress (to garnish) — optional
French dressing (see page 137)

A curd cheese such as Gervais
is best to use here as it is richer
than cottage cheese, but not as
rich as the Petit-Suisse type of
full cream cheese.

If neither fresh chives nor the
A.F.D. (accelerated freeze dried)
ones are available and the alter-
natives suggested above are
used, then chopped herbs, such
as thyme, marjoram or basil,
should be added to the dressing.

Method

Scald and skin the tomatoes.
Drain and lightly season inside
each one with salt.

Sieve the cheese by pushing
it through a strainer resting on a
bowl, using a wooden spoon or
plastic spatula. Season well and
add some of the chives (cut
finely with scissors), or chopped
herbs. Soften with cream or top
of the milk.

Fill the tomatoes with this
cheese mixture with a teaspoon,
replace their top slices on the
slant and arrange them in a
serving dish.

Make the French dressing
and spoon a little over tomatoes (be sure to reserve some
for spooning over at the last
moment). Chill for up to 2 hours
before serving. Garnish with
watercress and sprinkle remains
of chives over tomatoes. Serve
with brown bread and butter.

> **To skin tomatoes,** scald by
> placing in a bowl, pouring
> boiling water over them,
> counting 12 before pouring
> off the hot water and replac-
> ing it with cold. The skin
> then comes off easily.
> **To remove seeds,** cut a slice
> from the top (not stalk end)
> of each tomato, hold tomato
> in hollow of your palm, flick
> out seeds with the handle
> of a teaspoon, using the
> bowl of the spoon to detach
> the core. So much the better
> if the spoon is worn and
> therefore slightly sharp.

Chicken Véronique

3-3½ lb roasting chicken
salt and pepper
2 oz butter
3-4 sprigs tarragon
½ pint chicken stock (see page 139)
½-1 teaspoon arrowroot
2-3 tablespoons double cream
4 oz muscat, or other white grapes
(peeled and pipped)
squeeze of lemon juice

Method

Set the oven at 400°F or Mark 6. Wipe the chicken inside with a damp cloth but do not wash the bird as this would hinder browning and do nothing to improve its flavour. Season inside as this will penetrate the flesh, whereas seasoning on the outside only would not, and the salt would draw out the juices and prevent browning.

Truss the chicken and rub well with 2 oz of butter, putting a good nut of this inside with the tarragon and seasoning. Place the chicken, breast side up, in the roasting tin, with half of the chicken stock. Cover with buttered paper. Roast for about 1 hour in pre-set oven.

After the first 15-20 minutes, when the flesh should be set but not coloured, baste and turn on one side. Baste and turn again after another 15-20 minutes and finish off with breast side up again, removing the buttered paper for the last few minutes of roasting. The chicken should be well browned on all sides. This method of cooking is known as French roasting.

To test if the chicken is done, take a cooking knife with a fine point (or even a hat pin) and pierce the flesh of the thigh. The liquid that runs out should be quite clear ; continue cooking if it is at all pink. A frozen bird usually takes longer to cook and colour because the skin is so wet.

When cooked, take chicken out of oven, carve on a wooden board and keep hot. If, at the end of cooking time, the juices in the pan have not cooked down to a glaze (a sticky consistency), put tin over steady heat on top of stove, leaving juices and butter to reduce until brown and sticky. Then add remaining ¼ pint of stock (or water) to make gravy.

Scrape the pan well with the basting spoon and strain mixture into a small saucepan. To thicken slightly, so as to bind the butter into the stock, add ½-1 teaspoon of arrowroot (mixed with 1 tablespoon of stock or water). Add this away from the heat and then stir until boiling. It needs no further cooking and will be quite clear. Mix in the cream, adjust the seasoning to taste, and keep hot.

If grapes are difficult to peel, scald by pouring water over them, count 12, then replace hot water with cold. Then peel and pip them, cover with a little lemon juice and wet, greaseproof paper to keep out air until they are needed.

When chicken, gravy and potatoes are ready to be dished up, turn out the potato cake to form a bed on which to arrange the served pieces of chicken. Put grapes into the gravy and spoon them over the chicken with as much liquid as comes with them. Serve the rest of the gravy in a sauce boat, otherwise you will find the potatoes soak up all of the sauce. (Recipe for potato cake is overleaf.)

▶ 27

Chicken Véronique continued

Chicken Véronique is just one way to turn an ordinary roast chicken into something special. Served in a rich gravy made with cream and garnished with grapes, it is dished up on a crisp julienne potato cake

Julienne potato cake

1 lb potatoes (peeled)
1 oz butter
salt and pepper

Method

Although the potatoes may be peeled ahead of time, they must never be cut into strips until you are ready to cook them. Soaking in water removes a certain amount of their starch which is needed to knit them together.

Cut the peeled potatoes into julienne strips. Dry well in a cloth or absorbent kitchen paper.

A heavy 6-inch diameter frying pan is ideal for these as a larger one makes it almost impossible to turn out the potato cake. Rub a thick, even coating of butter (1 oz) over the base and sides of the pan, press in the potatoes, season only when a thick layer covers the base, or the salt will make the potatoes stick. All the seasoning will be absorbed by the potatoes, none being thrown away as with the liquid from boiled potatoes.

If lid is not close-fitting, put a layer of overlapping, buttered paper between pan and lid to prevent loss of steam as this would result in potatoes over-browning or burning on the bottom before they are quite tender.

If cooked on top of stove, heat must be gentle and even (allow about 30-40 minutes). Alternatively combine top of stove and oven heat for cooking in following way.

Cook for about 10-15 minutes on top of stove on a steady heat, testing colouring of strips by lifting lid, inserting a palette knife down side and taking a quick look. With experience your nose will tell you when potatoes are coloured by the unmistakable smell of beurre noisette (butter cooked to a nut-brown). At this stage transfer pan to oven below chicken if oven is still set at 400°F or Mark 6, or above if chicken is cooked and oven has been turned low. Continue cooking for about 30 minutes. For final testing to see if done, use the point of a cooking knife.

If you want to make larger quantities than for 4-6 people, use 2 sandwich tins and lids made from foil with a plate on top. The pan or tin should be generously full, the weight of the plate (in the case of the tin) being used to press the potatoes down. In this case cook on top for 10 minutes only, finishing off in oven as above.

The potato cake is turned out for serving, browned side up, with the Chicken Véronique (see opposite)

Green salad

The classic accompaniment to a French roast chicken is a green salad mixed with a French dressing (see page 137) and liberally sprinkled with chopped herbs and parsley.

Green salads can be of plain lettuce — cabbage, cos, Webb's or Iceberg — depending on the season, or be a mixture of salad greens, such as watercress, sliced cucumber and spring onions. Chicory can also be added in season, but tomato and beetroot (which normally go into an English salad) are best served separately.

Preparation of the salad greens is of great importance. Lettuce leaves should be carefully detached and the outside coarse ones discarded. A fruit or stainless steel knife (not a carbon knife) may be used to trim the bottom stalk, or to quarter the hearts if using them for garnish. If the leaves are too large, pull rather than cut them apart. Wash them well, then swing dry in a salad basket or clean muslin cloth. Make sure this is thoroughly done. If lettuce is at all limp, put it into the refrigerator (in the salad drawer or hydrator) until crisp.

Watercress should be well rinsed in the bunch under the cold tap, then shaken to get rid of the moisture. Carefully pick over and remove some of the stalk, but if this is clean (ie. free from any little hairs) do not discard. These stalks can be snipped into little pieces with scissors and used with chopped herbs, or scattered over vegetable soups, or for a savoury butter. They have a pleasant, slightly peppery taste.

Garlic may be used to flavour, but use it cautiously in a green salad. Either rub the bowl with a peeled clove, or better still, rub a clove well over a crust of French or ordinary bread. Having put the salad into the bowl, bury this chapon, as it is called, among the leaves (not forgetting to remove it before serving the salad at the table).

A green salad should be dressed at the last moment, otherwise the leaves will wilt and be unappetising. For a large amount of salad, you will find it easier to mix with its dressing in a really big bowl, and then to transfer it to your salad bowl.

There is, however, a way of dressing the salad where the leaves remain crisp for slightly longer. Sprinkle in enough oil on its own, tossing the leaves all the time to make them glisten. Mix the vinegar (a third of the quantity of oil used) and seasoning together, and sprinkle over the bowl. For a stronger flavour crush garlic with a little salt and add to this dressing. Stir once or twice before serving the salad, so that the dressing is evenly distributed.

Salad vegetables and herbs, from left to right, front : cucumber, green pepper, cabbage lettuce, chicory (English), Cos lettuce. Behind : watercress. thyme, chives, mint, parsley, garlic, endive (English), Webb's Wonder lettuce in collapsible salad basket

Chocolate mousse basque

6 oz plain block chocolate
2-3 tablespoons water, or black coffee
$\frac{1}{2}$ oz butter
1 dessertspoon rum, or 2-3 drops vanilla essence
3 eggs
1 small carton (2$\frac{1}{2}$ fl oz) double cream

4-6 mousse or custard pots

Method
Break the chocolate into small pieces, put into a pan with the liquid and stir continually over a gentle heat to a thick cream. The chocolate should be hot but the sides of the pan never so hot that you cannot touch them. Take off the heat, stir in the butter and flavouring.

Crack each of the eggs, putting the whites into a basin and dropping the yolks, one at a time, into the chocolate pan ; stir well after each addition.

Watchpoint It is important that the chocolate is hot when the yolks go in so that they get slightly cooked.

Whisk the whites to a firm snow, then stir briskly into the chocolate. When thoroughly mixed fill the small pots and leave overnight in the larder or refrigerator. For easy pouring turn the mixture first into a jug, scraping the pan out well. These mousses may be served plain with special biscuits, or a blob of whipped cream can be spooned, or piped (with an 8-cut rose pipe and forcing bag, preferably of nylon), on top of each mousse. If cream is used, you could stick a biscuit, such as a cigarette russe, in the centre of each one just before, serving.

Cigarettes russes

2 egg whites
4 oz caster sugar
2 oz butter
2 oz plain flour (sifted)
2-3 drops of vanilla essence

Method
Set oven at 400°F or Mark 6. Break up the egg whites in a basin, add the sugar and beat with a fork until smooth. Melt the butter and add with the sifted flour to the mixture. Flavour with 2-3 drops of vanilla essence.

Spread the mixture in oblongs on the greased and floured baking sheet and bake for 5-6 minutes in pre-set oven. (It is a good idea to test mixture by baking one only at first. If difficult to handle, add a pinch of flour, or if too firm and hard, you can add 1 dessertspoon of melted butter).

Take the oblongs out of the oven and allow to stand for 1-2 seconds, then remove them with a sharp knife, placing them upside down on the table. Roll each one tightly round a wooden spoon handle, skewer or pencil, holding it firmly with your hand. Remove at once from the spoon, and allow to cool. Store in an airtight tin.

Ready to serve, chocolate mousse basque with cigarettes russes

Menu 5 Lobster

Starter : Iced cucumber soup

Main course : Lobster thermidor with French beans

Dessert : Fresh fruit salad with almond biscuits

TIMETABLE

Day before
Make soup and store covered
in refrigerator.
Make and bake almond
biscuits ; when cold store
in airtight container.

Morning
Prepare lobsters and leave
ready for browning.
Prepare fresh fruit salad,
cover, and chill in
refrigerator.
Assemble equipment for
final cooking from 7.30 for
dinner around 8 pm.

Order of work
7.30 Set oven.

7.40 Put lobsters to brown
in oven. Cook French
beans.
Add cream and mint
to soup.

7.55 Turn gas oven to lowest
setting or electric
oven off.
Drain beans, toss in
butter and keep warm.

8.00 Serve first course.

Iced cucumber soup

2 medium-size cucumbers
2 shallots, or 1 medium-size onion
  (finely chopped)
3 pints chicken stock (see page 139)
2 oz butter
2 tablespoons plain flour
salt and pepper
3 eggs yolks
6-8 tablespoons double cream
2-3 drops of green edible colouring

To garnish
3 tablespoons double cream
  (very lightly whipped)
1 tablespoon finely chopped mint,
  or chives

Adding some of the hot soup to liaison of egg yolks and cream before blending it in

Method
Peel cucumbers and cut into $\frac{1}{2}$ inch slices ; simmer in a pan with shallot and stock for 15-20 minutes until soft. Rub through a nylon strainer or work in a liquidiser until smooth. Melt the butter, add the flour and cook until straw-coloured and marbled in appearance. Blend in the cucumber liquid, stir until boiling, then season and simmer for 2-3 minutes.

Work the yolks and cream together in a bowl with a wooden spoon, draw the soup off the heat and then very slowly add about 3-4 tablespoons of the hot soup to this liaison. Return this to the saucepan a little at a time, then reheat gently without boiling until the soup has thickened. Colour the soup very delicately, adjust seasoning and pour into a container ready for chilling. Cover soup to prevent a skin forming and when cold place it in refrigerator or in a bowl packed with ice to chill.

Remember to chill the tureen and soup cups before serving. Put a rounded teaspoon of cream in each cup, or the equivalent in a tureen, and stir it in gently to give the soup a streaky look ; sprinkle with mint or chives.

Lobster thermidor

2 live lobsters (about ¾-1 lb each)
2 tablespoons oil
1½ oz butter
béchamel sauce (made with 1 oz
    butter, scant 1 oz plain flour, 7½ fl
    oz flavoured milk — see method,
    page 138)
2 shallots (finely chopped)
1 wineglass dry white wine
1 teaspoon each chopped tarragon
    and chervil, or pinch of dried
    herbs
2 tablespoons double cream
½ teaspoon French mustard
2 tablespoons grated Parmesan
    cheese
salt and pepper

To finish
browned crumbs
melted butter
watercress

Method

Kill and split lobsters (see page 134), remove sac and intestine. Have ready the oil and 1 oz of the butter, heated in a sauté pan. Put in the lobster, cut side down, cover pan and cook gently for 12-15 minutes or until the lobster is red. Turn once only.

Make béchamel sauce and set aside in pan. Put shallot in a smaller saucepan with rest of butter, cook for ½ minute then add wine and herbs. Reduce to half quantity then add to the béchamel sauce. Set this mixture on low heat.

Take out the lobsters and strain any juice into the sauce. Stir well, add cream. Simmer for 2-3 minutes, then draw aside and mix in mustard and half the cheese. Season, cover pan and leave off heat.

Take out lobster meat, coarsely chopping claw meat and slicing tail into 'scallops' Add 1-2 tablespoons of sauce to the claw meat and put into the head shells. Put 1 tablespoon of sauce into the tail shells and replace 'scallops',

Splitting the uncooked lobsters

Coating cooked lobsters with sauce

rounded side up. Place shells on a baking sheet, wedging them with a piece of potato or on circles of claws. Coat lobster with rest of sauce, sprinkle with crumbs, rest of cheese and a little melted butter. Brown in the oven at 400°F or Mark 6 for 7-10 minutes. Garnish with watercress and serve very hot on a napkin.

Note : if there is coral (spawn) in the lobster, remove after splitting. Work on a plate with a palette knife, adding about $\frac{1}{2}$ oz butter, then rub through a bowl strainer. Lobster thermidor does not have coral added but if you have no other immediate use for it (such as for a soup) add it to the sauce with the cream.

Fresh fruit salad

2 oranges
2 clementines
3 ripe pears
8 oz grapes
3 bananas

For sugar syrup
3 oz granulated sugar
1 strip of lemon rind, or piece of vanilla pod
6 tablespoons water
2-3 tablespoons liqueur (kirsch, or maraschino) — optional

Method

First prepare sugar syrup : dissolve sugar slowly in the water, add lemon rind or vanilla pod, and boil for 1 minute. Tip into a bowl and leave to cool. Remove lemon rind (or vanilla pod).

Cut peel, pith and first skin from oranges with a sharp, serrated-edge knife to expose flesh ; then remove segments by cutting between each membrane. Peel and slice clementines. Peel and quarter pears, remove core, cut each quarter into two. Pip grapes by hooking out pips with eye of a trussing needle. Only white grapes should be peeled, not black ones. If skin is difficult to remove from white grapes, dip them into boiling water for 1 minute. Peel bananas and cut in thick, slanting slices.

Moisten fruit with sugar syrup, add liqueur and turn fruit over carefully. Set a plate on top to keep fruit covered by the syrup. Chill before serving.

Curling the cooked almond biscuits round a rolling pin while warm ; if allowed to get too cool, they will break when you try to mould them

Almond biscuits

3 oz butter
3 oz caster sugar
2 oz plain flour
pinch of salt
3 oz almonds (finely shredded)

These biscuits are known as 'tuiles' because they resemble curved tiles.

Method

Set the oven at 400°F or Mark 6. Soften butter, add sugar and beat well with wooden spoon until light and fluffy. Sift flour with a pinch of salt and stir into the mixture with the almonds. Put mixture a teaspoon at a time on to a well-greased baking tin and flatten with a wet fork.

Watchpoint Leave plenty of space between the biscuits as they will spread during cooking.

Bake in the oven until just coloured (6-8 minutes). Allow to stand a second or two before removing from the tin with a sharp knife. Curl on a rolling pin until set. Store when cool in an airtight container.

Menu 6 Scampi

Starter : Melon salad with hot herb loaf

Main course : Scampi provençale with boiled rice

Dessert : Cassata

TIMETABLE

Day before
Prepare cassata and store
in home freezer or
ice-making compartment
of refrigerator.
Prepare herb loaf ; wrap
in foil ready for baking.

Morning
Cook rice, drain and dry and
place in buttered dish ready
for reheating.
Prepare sauce for scampi.
Wash and slice mushrooms
and prepare tomatoes for
scampi.

Assemble ingredients and
equipment for final cooking
from 5.00 for dinner
around 8 pm.

Order of work

5.00 Prepare melon salad,
cover and put in
refrigerator to chill.

7.00 Set oven at 425°F or
Mark 7. Put herb loaf
to bake. After 10 min-
utes reduce oven
setting to 400°F or
Mark 6. Put rice to heat.
Fry scampi, then
mushrooms ; add sauce
and tomatoes and
simmer for 1 minute.
Keep hot.

7.55 Dip bombe in cold water
and turn out. Keep in
refrigerator until ready
to serve.

8.00 Serve first course.

Melon salad

1 honeydew melon
1 lb tomatoes
1 large cucumber
salt
1 tablespoon chopped parsley
1 heaped teaspoon chopped mint
   and chives

For French dressing
2 tablespoons wine vinegar
salt and pepper
caster sugar
6 tablespoons salad oil

Method
Cut the melon in half, remove the seeds and scoop out the flesh with a vegetable cutter or cut into cubes.

Skin and quarter the tomatoes (see page 26), squeeze out the seeds and remove the core ; cut quarters again if the tomatoes are large.

Peel the cucumber, cut in small cubes, or the same size as the melon cubes. Sprinkle lightly with salt, cover with a plate and stand for 30 minutes ; drain away any liquid and rinse cubes with cold water.

To prepare the dressing : mix the vinegar, seasoning and sugar together, whisk in oil.

Mix the melon and vegetables together in a deep bowl (or soup tureen), pour over the dressing, cover and chill for 2-3 hours.

Just before serving, mix in the herbs. Serve from the bowl or tureen with a ladle into soup cups.

While standing, the salad will make a lot of juice, so it should be eaten with a spoon. You'll find a hot herb loaf goes well with melon salad.

Hot herb loaf

1 French loaf
4 oz butter
1 tablespoon mixed dried herbs
juice of $\frac{1}{4}$ lemon
black pepper
little garlic (crushed) — optional

Method
Cream the butter with the herbs, lemon juice and seasoning ; if you like garlic, add a little now.

Cut the loaf in even, slanting slices about $\frac{1}{2}$ inch thick ; spread each slice generously with the butter mixture and reshape the loaf, spreading any remaining butter over the top and sides before wrapping in foil.

Bake for 10 minutes in a hot oven at 425°F or Mark 7. Then reduce oven setting to 400°F or Mark 6, and open the foil so that the bread browns and crisps. This should take a further 5-8 minutes.

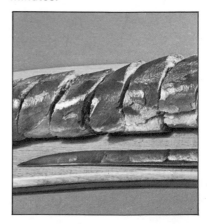

Scampi provençale

1 lb scampi
seasoned flour
1 oz butter (to sauté)
3 oz button mushrooms (sliced)
3 tomatoes (skinned, hard stalk and
    seeds removed — see page 26)
5 oz boiled long grain rice (for
    serving) — see page 137

For sauce
2 shallots (finely chopped)
bouquet garni
1 wineglass white wine
1 oz butter
½ oz plain flour
1 clove of garlic (crushed with
    ½ teaspoon salt)
1 teaspoon tomato purée
½ pint good stock (see page 139)

Method
Prepare the sauce. Simmer shallots with bouquet garni and wine until liquor is reduced by half, then remove bouquet garni and set sauce aside.

Melt ½ oz butter, add flour, brown lightly, then add garlic, tomato purée and stock. Simmer for 10-15 minutes, then pour in reduced wine and cook a further 5 minutes. Draw aside and add small shavings of butter. Keep hot.

Roll scampi in seasoned flour and sauté lightly in 1 oz butter for 5-6 minutes. Lift into serving dish. Sauté the mushrooms in the pan and add to the sauce with the tomatoes, roughly chopped. Reboil for 1 minute, then spoon over scampi. Serve with rice.

Cassata

1 **pint vanilla cream ice (see page 121)**
1 **pint chocolate cream ice (see page 122)**
$\frac{1}{4}$ **pint double cream (whipped)**
4-5 **tablespoons mixed chopped glacé fruit (soaked in 2 tablespoons rum)**

Bombe mould ($1\frac{1}{4}$-$1\frac{1}{2}$ pints capacity), or 7-8 inch diameter cake tin

Method

Have the well-chilled mould or tin ready. Line it with the vanilla cream ice, then line again with the chocolate cream ice ; keep some vanilla cream ice aside for the centre. Fill the centre with the macerated glacé fruit mixed with the whipped cream and cover with the remaining cream ice. Put a piece of foil over top and freeze, preferably in a home-freezer for 6 hours, or overnight in the ice-making compartment of a refrigerator turned to its lowest temperature.

To serve, dip the bombe or tin into cold water and turn cut the cassata. Cut it into slices.

Menu 7 Chicken

Starter : Gratin of seafood

Main course : Fried chicken with sweetcorn fritters and green salad with fresh pineapple

Dessert : Caramel and vanilla bavarois

TIMETABLE

Morning
Prepare both custards for bavarois (but do not add gelatine yet), and leave to cool.
Make breadcrumbs to coat chicken and for fritters.
Joint chicken. Make chicken stock from giblets and joint trimmings.
Cook frozen sweetcorn or drain canned variety.
Wash lettuce, wrap in cloth and leave to crisp in refrigerator.
Cut pineapple and sprinkle with sugar.
Make French dressing, pour a little on to pineapple.
Chop parsley.
Remove rind and rust from bacon.
Add gelatine to both custards for bavarois, fold in whipped cream and put mixtures into tin when they begin to set.
Cover with foil and keep in refrigerator or cool place.
Make caramel decoration and sauce.
Prepare fish, coat with sauce and sprinkle with cheese but do not bake yet.

Assemble equipment for final cooking from 6.15 for dinner around 8 pm.

Order of work

6.15 Turn out bavarois and decorate. Egg and breadcrumb chicken. Make sauce for chicken and keep warm in double saucepan or bowl over hot water. Prepare sweetcorn fritter mixture.

7.00 Set oven at 350°F or Mark 4. Put plates and dishes to warm.
Fry fritters — leave on crumpled absorbent paper in warming drawer or at very bottom of gas oven.
Start frying, or grilling, chicken.

7.30 Put fish in oven.
Whisk French dressing, toss lettuce and dish up salad.
Grill bacon, dish up chicken and garnish with bacon and fritters. Keep hot.

8.00 Serve first course.

43

Gratin of seafood

1¼ lb cod fillet, or 4 frozen cod steaks
juice of ½ lemon
2 oz button mushrooms
4 oz prawns (shelled)
½ pint milk
slice of onion
6 peppercorns
blade of mace
1 oz butter
1 oz plain flour
salt and pepper
1 tablespoon grated Parmesan
cheese

4 individual gratin dishes

Method
Set the oven at 350°F or Mark 4. If using fresh cod, discard the skin and cut fillets into fine strips. Grease 4 individual ovenproof gratin dishes (preferably with butter), put in fish and sprinkle with lemon juice. If using frozen cod, thaw, place in gratin dishes and sprinkle with lemon juice.

Wash mushrooms quickly in salted water, trim away stalks and then cut in fine slices. Sprinkle mushrooms and prawns on to the fish strips.

Put milk in a pan with the onion, peppercorns and mace, warm and remove from heat. Cover pan and leave to infuse until milk is well flavoured (at least 15 minutes). Strain.

Melt butter in a saucepan, remove pan from heat and blend in flour and flavoured milk. Season, stir over gentle heat until boiling, then simmer for 1 minute. Adjust the seasoning.

Spoon sauce over the fish, sprinkle with Parmesan cheese, bake for 20-25 minutes in pre-set oven until golden-brown.

Fried (or grilled) chicken
with sweetcorn fritters

6-8 chicken joints (breast and
    wing joints), or 2 young chickens
2 tablespoons seasoned flour
1 egg (beaten)
1 tablespoon oil
1 cup of fresh white breadcrumbs
4 oz clarified butter

For sweetcorn fritters
1 cup of cooked frozen, or canned,
    sweetcorn kernels
2 eggs
salt and pepper
pinch of caster sugar
1 teaspoon baking powder
$\frac{1}{2}$-1 cup of fresh white breadcrumbs
oil (for frying)

For sauce
1 oz butter
1 rounded tablespoon plain flour
$\frac{3}{4}$ cup of chicken stock (see page 139)
    or bouillon cube with water
salt and pepper
1 dessertspoon grated horseradish
squeeze of lemon juice
5 tablespoons single cream

For garnish
8 rashers of streaky bacon

Method

If using whole chickens, joint
and trim them. Roll in seasoned
flour.

Mix the beaten egg with the
oil (this keeps chicken moist)
and brush the chicken joints
with it. Roll joints in the breadcrumbs and press them on
firmly with a palette knife.

To prepare fritters : separate
the eggs, beat yolks well with
the seasoning and sugar and
then add the sweetcorn. Beat
egg whites until stiff and fold
into the sweetcorn with the
baking powder and enough
breadcrumbs to bring mixture
to a dropping consistency.

Heat the oil (enough to give
a depth of $\frac{1}{4}$ inch in the frying
pan), drop in sweetcorn mixture,
a dessertspoon at a time, and
fry until golden-brown on one
side before turning and
browning on the other side. Then
lift out with a draining spoon,
leave on crumpled absorbent
paper in warming drawer or at
bottom of oven.

To prepare sauce : melt the
butter in a pan, stir in flour and
cook gently until a pale straw
colour ; remove from the heat,
blend in stock and season to
taste. Stir over gentle heat until
boiling, simmer for 2-3 minutes,
then add the horseradish, lemon
juice and cream. Keep warm.

To fry chicken : heat the
clarified butter in a large frying
pan, arrange pieces of chicken
in this and fry gently, turning
occasionally so that they are
well browned on all sides.

If you prefer to grill the joints,
baste well with heated, clarified
butter before and during cooking.
When cooked, arrange in a hot
dish with fritters and keep
warm.

To garnish ; remove rind from
the bacon, fry or grill and
arrange round the chicken.
Serve the sauce separately.

Green salad
with fresh pineapple

1 lettuce
1 small fresh pineapple
1 tablespoon caster sugar

For French dressing
2 tablespoons wine vinegar
salt
pepper (ground from mill)
6 tablespoons salad oil
1 teaspoon chopped parsley
(optional)

Method

Cut the skin from the pineapple, slice the flesh and discard the core. Sprinkle with sugar. Leave for at least 30 minutes.

Wash lettuce, drain, wrap in a clean tea towel or a paper towel, then leave in the refrigerator to get really crisp. If you haven't a refrigerator, leave preparation of the lettuce until the last minute or it will become soft and limp.

To prepare French dressing : add seasoning to vinegar and whisk in the oil gradually until mixture emulsifies. Taste and adjust seasoning. Pour a little dressing over the pineapple.

Just before serving, put lettuce leaves in a salad bowl and toss them in enough dressing to coat each leaf. Add pineapple to the lettuce, sprinkle with parsley and serve at once.

To peel and cut fresh pineapple : slice bottom off with a serrated-edge knife, hold the pineapple firmly and cut downwards between 'eyes' at an angle of about 45° with a sharp, stainless steel knife. These eyes should then come out easily in strips. Now remove the top, slice the flesh and remove core with a grapefruit knife. This method of peeling and coring will avoid waste.

Caramel and vanilla bavarois

For caramel custard mixture
4 oz lump, or granulated, sugar
$\frac{1}{4}$ pint water
$\frac{1}{2}$ pint milk
3 egg yolks
1$\frac{1}{2}$ oz caster sugar
$\frac{1}{2}$ oz gelatine
5 tablespoons water

For vanilla custard mixture
1 vanilla pod, or 2-3 drops of
  vanilla essence
$\frac{3}{4}$ pint milk
3 egg yolks
1$\frac{1}{2}$ oz caster sugar
$\frac{1}{2}$ oz gelatine
5 tablespoons water

$\frac{1}{4}$ pint double cream

For sauce and decoration
6 oz lump, or granulated, sugar
$\frac{3}{4}$ cup of water
$\frac{1}{4}$ pint double cream

*8-inch diameter angel cake tin ;
baking tin or enamel plate, for
caramel decoration*

An angel cake tin (a round
tin with a hollow centre) is particularly effective for this dish,
but an ordinary deep, round
mould can be used.
Quantities given here will
make 1$\frac{1}{2}$ pints — enough for 6.

> **Bavarian cream** (bavarois)
> it is a rich egg custard
> stiffened or set with ge-
> latine, with whipped cream
> added.

Method

To prepare caramel custard :
put half the $\frac{1}{4}$ pint of water in a
saucepan, dissolve lump or
granulated sugar slowly in it and
boil steadily until a rich brown
caramel. Pour on remaining
water and stir until caramel is
dissolved; stir in milk.
Watchpoint For protection when
adding the water, cover the hand
holding the pan with a cloth or
glove because the mixture will
sizzle furiously.
    Cream egg yolks and caster
sugar together in a basin until
light, stir in caramel flavoured
milk, return to the saucepan and
thicken custard over a gentle
heat without letting it boil.
Watchpoint On no account must
the mixture boil or the eggs will
curdle.
    Strain custard into a metal
pan and cool.
    Meanwhile, prepare vanilla
custard : put milk in a pan with
the vanilla pod (if using one),
bring barely to the boil and
leave to infuse. Cream egg yolks
with the sugar until light, stir in
the milk (removing vanilla pod),
and thicken in a small saucepan
over a gentle heat without
boiling. Strain and cool in a
metal pan. If using vanilla
essence, stir it in at this point.
    Soak gelatine for caramel
custard in the 5 tablespoons of
water, dissolve over a gentle
heat, add to custard and set
aside. Soak gelatine for vanilla
custard in water, dissolve over a
gentle heat, add to custard and
set aside. Lightly whip the $\frac{1}{4}$ pint
of cream in a basin.
    Set the saucepan of caramel
custard in a bowl containing
cold water and 2-3 ice cubes
and stir until the custard begins

to set. (A metal saucepan responds to temperature changes more quickly than a pottery bowl, so custard sets faster if kept in saucepan.)

Watchpoint It is important to stir from time to time or the custard mixture will not set smoothly.

Fold in half the whipped cream and pour caramel custard mixture into the lightly-oiled cake tin.

Cool vanilla custard in the same way and fold in remainder of whipped cream as custard begins to set.

Pour the vanilla custard into the cake tin, swirling a knife through the two mixtures to give a marbled effect. (Cake tin will not be full to top.) Leave in a cool place to set.

To prepare sauce : dissolve sugar in half the water, boil steadily to a rich brown caramel and then pour a little on to the oiled tin or plate. Leave to set, and keep for decoration. Meanwhile slowly add the rest of the water to caramel remaining in the saucepan (not forgetting to

cover with a cloth the hand with which you hold the pan while the mixture sizzles). Stir carefully until caramel has dissolved. Pour sauce into a basin and leave to cool.

Turn out bavarois on to a serving dish. To do this, loosen sides with a palette or table knife, easing the knife down to the bottom at one spot and letting in a little air to release the vacuum. Put the serving plate over the top of the tin and turn over. Hold plate and tin and shake once or twice from side to side, when the bavarois should slide out quite easily.

Watchpoint Never dip a creamy sweet in hot water to loosen as this spoils the appearance ; it is only done for jellies which are much firmer mixtures.

For decoration : whip remaining $\frac{1}{4}$ pint of cream until firm enough to pipe. Crush sheet of caramel (from tin or enamel plate) into small pieces. Pipe rosettes of whipped cream over the bavarois and decorate with crushed caramel. Serve sauce separately.

Menu 8 Ham

Starter : Hors d'œuvre

Main course : Ham mousse, with basque salad

Dessert : Hazelnut meringue cake, with Melba sauce

TIMETABLE

Day before
Prepare and make mousse.
Make hazelnut meringue
cake and Melba sauce, but
do not fill cake.

Morning
Prepare hors d'œuvre,
cover and keep in a
cool place.
Prepare peppers and
tomatoes for salad.
Make dressing.
Assemble equipment for
final preparation from 5 pm.

Order of work
5.00 Fill and decorate cake.
Make and complete
salad.
The menu is then ready
for serving at 7.30 or
8.00, as you prefer.

Hors d'œuvre

The hors d'œuvre course should consist of two or three 'straight' dishes — slices of salami, garlic or liver sausage — together with two or three salads dressed with a mayonnaise or vinaigrette dressing such as those given below.

Mushrooms Philippe

4-6 oz button mushrooms
1 large tablespoon olive oil
1 shallot (finely chopped)
1 wineglass red wine
1 teaspoon freshly chopped thyme
1-2 tablespoons French dressing (preferably made with red wine vinegar — see page 137)
salt and pepper

Method
Wash and trim mushrooms (cut off stalks level with caps, slice stalks lengthways and put with mushroom caps).

Heat oil in a small frying pan, put in the mushrooms and the shallot. Fry briskly for about 3 minutes, turning and stirring them all the time.

Lift out mushroom mixture with a draining spoon into a bowl. Pour wine into the pan and boil until it is reduced by half. Add to the mushrooms with the herbs and French dressing. Season well, cover, and leave until cold.

Herring and dill cucumber salad

2-3 preserved herring fillets
1 Spanish onion (sliced)
2 dill cucumbers (sliced)
French dressing (made with dry white wine instead of vinegar — see page 137)

Method
Cut fillets into strips diagonally. Set aside. Push onion slices out into rings. Blanch for 5-6 minutes, then drain and refresh.

Arrange herring fillets in centre of serving dish, surround with the cucumber and place the onion round that. Spoon over enough French dressing to moisten well.

Anchovy and bean salad

2-3 oz haricot, or buttered, beans (well soaked and simmered until tender), or 1 can butter beans (drained from their liquid)
1 small can anchovy fillets

For dressing
$\frac{1}{2}$ teaspoon grated onion
$\frac{1}{2}$ tablespoon white wine vinegar
2 tablespoons oil
1 teaspoon anchovy essence
2 tablespoons double cream
1 dessertspoon chopped parsley

Method
Combine all ingredients for the dressing, mix with the beans. Put salad in serving dish. Have ready the anchovy fillets, split in two lengthways. Arrange these lattice-fashion over salad.

Ham mousse

½ lb ham (cooked)
½ pint sauce madère (see page 139)
salt and pepper
½ oz gelatine
2 tablespoons stock
¼ pint aspic jelly (see page 132)
2-3 drops carmine (optional)
¼ pint double cream (lightly whipped)

For decoration
2½ fl oz aspic jelly
1 tablespoon chopped truffle, or
  chopped, cooked mushroom

*5½-inch diameter top (size No. 3)
soufflé dish*

Method
Prepare the soufflé dish with a band of greaseproof paper around the edge. Mince the ham twice, pound it well and sieve or work it in an electric blender with the sauce madère and seasoning.

Soak the gelatine in the stock, then add the aspic jelly and dissolve it over gentle heat. Add the colouring, if wished, and add all this to the ham mixture. Fold the whipped cream into the mixture. When mixture is on the point of setting, pour into prepared dish and leave to set.

To make decoration : add the chopped truffle (or mushroom) to the aspic jelly and pour over the top of the cold mousse, then chill it again. Remove the paper and serve mousse with basque salad.

Basque salad

3 red peppers
½ lb tomatoes
1 teaspoon caster sugar
1 French roll
1 teaspoon tomato purée
1 teaspoon paprika pepper
½ teaspoon black pepper
1 clove of garlic (crushed with
  ½ teaspoon salt)
2 tablespoons red wine vinegar
6 tablespoons olive oil

Method
Roast the peppers under a red-hot grill until the skin is charred all over. Rinse them under the cold tap and scrape well ; cut in half, scoop out the core and seeds, and shred flesh. Scald, skin and slice the tomatoes (see page 26) and dust very lightly with sugar.

Cut the French roll in $\frac{1}{2}$-inch slices and toast ; when cold put slices at the bottom of a large gratin dish.

For the dressing : mix the tomato purée, paprika, pepper and garlic together with wine vinegar and whisk in oil.

Place the peppers and tomatoes on the toast and spoon over the dressing.

Basque salad is served on small rounds of toast with ham mousse

Hazelnut meringue cake
with Melba sauce

4 egg whites
9 oz caster sugar
3-4 drops of vanilla essence
½ teaspoon vinegar
4½ oz hazelnuts (shelled,
   browned and ground)
¼ pint double cream
½ lb raspberries (fresh or frozen)
icing sugar (for dusting)

*Two 8-inch sandwich tins ; non-stick
  (silicone) cooking paper*

Method
Butter and flour the sides of the
sandwich tins and line the
bottom with a disc of non-stick
(silicone) cooking paper. Set the
oven at 375°F or Mark 5.

Whisk the egg whites until
stiff with a rotary or electric
beater, add the sugar 1 tablespoon at a time and continue
beating until the mixture is very
stiff and stands in peaks. Whisk
in the vanilla essence and
vinegar, then fold in prepared
nuts.

Divide the mixture between
the two prepared tins and
smooth the top with a palette

knife ; bake 30-40 minutes but no
longer. The top of the meringue
will be crisp and the inside soft
like a marshmallow. Turn on to
wire racks to cool.

Watchpoint Always fill meringue
at least three hours before
serving ; cake will then cut into
portions without splintering.

Whisk the cream, sweeten
and flavour with extra sugar and
vanilla ; use about two-thirds
to fill meringue. Pile raspberries
on top of the cream. Dust top
with icing sugar and use the
remaining cream to shape, or
pipe rosettes on the top. Serve
the Melba sauce separately.

Melba sauce

8 oz fresh raspberries, or frozen
   without sugar
4 tablespoons icing sugar (sifted)

Method
If buying frozen raspberries, get
them 1-2 days before you want
them and leave to thaw in the
refrigerator. Pick over the raspberries (if fresh), rub through a
nylon strainer and then beat the
sifted icing sugar into raspberry
purée 1 tablespoon at a time.

Picnics and barbecues

Picnics are a time for relaxing and carefree living, so match the food to the occasion. Modern packaging means you can carry almost any dish without damage, and you can keep ices cold or soups as hot as you can eat them. Whether you plan a detailed picnic menu or an informal selection of snacks, take some pretty paper tableware with you.

Even undomesticated friends will love to help you cook on a barbecue. The flavour of meat grilled over charcoal, and the delicious aroma that wafts around the garden, will make your barbecue party into an evening to be remembered.

Vegetable bortsch

beetroot
onions
carrots
celery
parsnip
salt and pepper
stock (preferably ham — see page
139), or water
cabbage (coarsely shredded)
garlic (chopped, or crushed) — to
taste
tomatoes
granulated sugar
little tomato purée
fresh parsley (chopped)

For liaison
little plain flour (optional)
soured cream

*5-inch diameter pudding basin
(sufficient for 3 pints liquid), or
small mixing bowl*

Quantities of vegetables should
be used in the following pro-
portions : half beetroot and of
remaining half, one-third onion,
one-third carrot and the last
third equally divided between
celery and parsnip.

> **To sour cream** at home,
> add the juice of $\frac{1}{2}$ lemon to
> 1 (5 fl oz) carton fresh
> cream.

Method
Cut beetroot, onions, carrots,
celery and parsnip into match-
sticks and pack into the basin
or bowl to fill it.

Lightly season stock or water
and bring to the boil. Turn the
bowl of vegetables into the pan,
cover and simmer for about
20-30 minutes. Coarsely shred
enough cabbage to fill the
bowl, add this with the garlic
to taste. Continue to simmer
gently, uncovered, for a further
20 minutes.

Skin sufficient tomatoes (see
page 26) to half-fill the bowl,
squeeze to remove seeds, then
chop flesh very coarsely. Add
to soup, season well with salt
and sugar and add a little
tomato purée to sharpen the
flavour. Simmer for a further 10
minutes, then add a handful of
chopped parsley.

The soup can be thickened
lightly with a little flour mixed
with a small quantity of soured
cream. Otherwise serve a bowl
of soured cream separately.

Watchpoint Bortsch should
be slightly piquant in flavour
and not sweet. Add salt and
sugar until this is reached. The
soup should be a thick broth of
vegetables but not too solid.
Dilute if necessary with additional stock.

This bortsch is improved if
made the previous day. On the
day of the picnic, reheat it and
put in a wide-necked vacuum jar.
If you use an ordinary vacuum
flask, make sure that the vegetables are cut into small enough
pieces and prepared with enough
fluid.

A colourful show of vegetables for making vegetable bortsch, a soup that is slightly piquant in taste

Smoked salmon or potted shrimps

Curl the salmon lightly and pack it in an airtight plastic container. If you have chosen potted shrimps, put the small plates in an insulated bag so that they will be warmed in readiness. Serve these with thin slices of Grant loaf (see page 71) or brown bread and butter and small quarters of lemon.

This picnic hamper includes rice salad, almond and raspberry flan and a selection of cheeses

Chicken mayonnaise

1 roasting, or boiling, chicken (4-5 lb)
root vegetables (to flavour) — sliced
bouquet garni
6-8 peppercorns
1 teaspoon salt
½-¾ pint mayonnaise (see page 137)
salt and pepper
lemon juice
strips of pimiento (to decorate)

This recipe serves 6 people.

Method
Place chicken in a large pan, add the root vegetables, bouquet garni, peppercorns and salt. Pour on enough cold water to come level with the top of the chicken legs, cover with a piece of foil or greaseproof paper and the lid. Set pan on a low heat and, after it has reached boiling point, simmer for 1¼-1½ hours, longer for a boiling fowl. Draw pan aside and cool chicken in the liquid.

When chicken is cold, take it out of the liquid, remove all skin and cut the meat from the carcass. Shred white and dark meat, keeping them separate ; arrange on a large tray or dish.

Season the mayonnaise well and sharpen it, if necessary, with a few drops of lemon juice. Spoon a good half of this over the chicken, lifting the pieces lightly with a fork to allow the mayonnaise to penetrate. Set aside.

When ready to pack for the picnic, arrange the chicken in a serving dish in layers of white and dark meat. Thin the rest of the mayonnaise, if necessary, and use it to coat the chicken. Decorate with strips of pimiento.

Rice salad

10 oz long grain rice (boiled and
   drained) — see page 137
1 large red carrot (diced)
4 oz French beans (diced)
1 teacup peas
½ cucumber
2 caps of pimiento, or 2-3
   tomatoes
French dressing (see page 137)

This recipe serves 6 people.

Method
Cook the carrot, French beans,
and peas separately in boiling
salted water until just tender,
then drain and refresh them.
Skin and dice cucumber, shred
the pimientos (or skin and shred
tomatoes). Add all the vegetables to the rice and fork up
with enough French dressing to
moisten.

Steak and kidney hot pot

1 ½ lb skirt, or shin, of beef
½ lb ox kidney
1 tablespoon dripping
1 rounded tablespoon plain flour
1 medium-size onion (finely
   chopped)
¼ lb mushrooms (sliced)
salt and pepper
¾ pint stock (see page 139)
1-1 ½ lb potatoes (peeled and
   sliced)
1-2 oz dripping, or butter

Method
Cut the meat into ½-inch dice
(small enough to be eaten with
a fork). Cut kidney the same
size, removing the core. Brown
the beef quickly in the dripping
and draw aside. Roll the kidney
in the flour. Pack meat, onion
and kidney into a thick casserole with the mushrooms and
plenty of seasoning. Pour on the
stock and cover casserole with
tight-fitting lid. Cook slowly on
top of the stove or in the oven,
pre-set at 325°F or Mark 3, for
2-3 hours or until the meat is
very tender.

After the first hour, cover the
top with a thick layer of
potatoes, dot with dripping
(or butter), cover again and
continue cooking. Remove lid
a good 30 minutes before the
meat is cooked to allow the
potatoes to become crusty.
Transfer to a wide-necked
vacuum jar for packing.

Almond and raspberry flan

½ lb fresh raspberries

For almond pastry
3 oz butter
1 oz shortening
6 oz plain flour
1½ oz ground almonds
1½ oz caster sugar
2-3 drops of vanilla essence
1 large egg yolk, or 2 small egg
  yolks
1-2 tablespoons cold water

For almond meringue
3 small egg whites
6 oz caster sugar
6 oz ground almonds

For decoration
½ pint double cream
caster sugar (to taste)
2-3 drops of vanilla essence
browned, shredded almonds (see
  page 134)

8-inch diameter flan ring

Method
First prepare almond pastry :
rub the fats into the flour, add
the ground almonds and sugar.
Mix the egg yolk(s) with vanilla
essence and water and add to
the dry ingredients. Work up
lightly to a firm paste and chill
for 15 minutes.

Set the oven at 350°F or
Mark 4. Line the flan ring with
the pastry, prick the bottom
lightly and cover with the
raspberries.

To prepare meringue : whip
the egg whites until frothy, add
the sugar a little at a time and
continue whisking until the
mixture stands in peaks. Fold
in the ground almonds. Spread
the almond mixture over the
raspberries and bake in the pre-
set moderate oven for about
30 minutes.

When the flan is cold, cover
it with the cream, lightly-
sweetened, whipped and
flavoured with vanilla essence ;
decorate with the browned
almonds.

*Covering the almond and raspberry
flan with whipped, flavoured cream*

Lemon whisky cake

3 eggs
weight of above eggs in butter,
   caster sugar, self-raising flour
   (well sifted)
6 oz sultanas (washed)
pared rind of 1 large lemon
2½ fl oz whisky

7-inch diameter cake tin

Method
Infuse the lemon rind in the whisky in a covered glass for 24 hours before use.

Prepare the cake tin by greasing and flouring. Set the oven at 350°F or Mark 4.

Cream the butter, add sugar gradually and beat until light and fluffy. Separate the eggs and add the yolks to the butter and sugar, one at a time, beating well. Stir in the sultanas, the strained whisky and half the flour.

Whip the egg whites to a firm snow and fold into the mixture with the remainder of the flour. Turn mixture into the tin and bake in the pre-set moderate oven for 50-60 minutes.

Adding whisky infusion to the lemon whisky cake mixture

Cheese board

You will obviously take along your own favourite cheeses, but no cheese board is complete without a chunk of good English Cheddar and one of the white English cheeses such as Caerphilly or Wensleydale. A ripe, moist Stilton will please your gourmet guests.

Among foreign cheeses, choose from the French Roquefort (made from ewes' milk) ; Dutch Edam or Gouda ; Swiss Gruyère or Emmenthal ; Italian Bel Paese, Gorgonzola or Mozzarella.

Pâté in aspic

4 oz calves liver
4 oz chicken, or pigs, liver
¼ pint béchamel sauce (see page 138)
pinch of mixed dried herbs
pinch of ground mace
salt and pepper
1 ham steak (3-3 ½ oz tender sweet
  bacon)
1 ½ pints aspic jelly (flavoured with
  sherry) — see page 132
tarragon leaves (for decoration)

8-10 ramekin dishes

Method

Prepare the béchamel sauce, flavour it with herbs and mace and season well ; turn on to a plate to cool. Set oven at 350°F or Mark 4.

Remove the fine skin and any ducts from the livers, cut in pieces and pass through a mincer. Mix the liver with the cold béchamel sauce and rub through a wire sieve or strainer, or work in a liquidiser, until smooth.

Cut the ham steak in ¼-inch cubes and fold into the liver mixture. Spoon the mixture into ramekin dishes until three-quarters full and tap them firmly on the table to settle the mixture and dispel any air bubbles.

Smooth the tops with a palette knife, cover each ramekin with foil or buttered paper. Stand them in a bain-marie and cook in pre-set oven for 40-45 minutes or until firm to the touch. Allow them to cool and keep in the refrigerator overnight.

The next day, wipe dishes carefully and fill to the top with cold but still liquid aspic, decorating each one with a tarragon leaf.

Salmon tourtière

2 lb salmon steak
4 oz long grain rice (boiled — see
  page 137)
4 hard-boiled eggs (chopped)
1 tablespoon chopped mixed herbs
salt and pepper
1 egg (beaten)
pinch of ground mace

For shortcrust pastry
12 oz plain flour
pinch of salt
3 oz butter
3 oz lard, or shortening
2 egg yolks
5-7 tablespoons water

*8-inch diameter shallow cake tin, or
  spring form mould, with loose
  bottom*

Method

Prepare the pastry (see method page 136).

Skin and bone the salmon, keeping the fillets whole. Chop any trimmings and mix with rice, chopped hard-boiled eggs, herbs, seasoning and beaten egg.

Set the oven at 400°F or Mark 6. Roll out the pastry, line into the cake tin, put a layer of the rice mixture on the bottom and set the fillets on this. Season with salt and pepper and ground mace. Cover with rest of rice and a 'lid' of the pastry. Seal and trim edges, brush with egg and decorate with any remaining pastry.

Bake in pre-set oven for 20-30 minutes, then lower heat to 350°F or Mark 4 and continue cooking for another 15-20 minutes. Remove from the oven and cool. Take out by pushing up the loose bottom of the tin ; avoid turning out if possible. Serve cold. (Pack in an airtight tin for travelling.)

Cucumber and tomato salad

1 cucumber
1 lb tomatoes
French dressing (see page 137)

Method

Peel the cucumber, cut it into chunks, salt lightly, cover and leave in a cool place for 1 hour. Scald and skin the tomatoes (see page 26) and cut each one into four, removing hard core and seeds. Tip off any liquid from the cucumber.

Prepare the French dressing. Mix the prepared vegetables together and moisten with the dressing. Pack in a tightly covered container.

Strawberries Cordon Bleu 1

1 lb strawberries
1 large orange
6-8 sugar lumps
1 small glass brandy (2 fl oz)

Method

Hull the strawberries and place them in a bowl. Rub the lumps of sugar over the rind of the orange until they are soaked with oil, then squeeze the juice from the orange. Crush the sugar cubes and mix them with the orange juice and brandy. Pour this syrup over the strawberries, place a plate on top and chill thoroughly (2-3 hours) before packing in an insulated container.

Strawberries Cordon Bleu 2

1 lb strawberries
$\frac{1}{4}$ lb ratafias, or 2 macaroons
grated rind and juice of 1 orange
1 tablespoon caster sugar
$\frac{1}{4}$ pint double cream

Method

Hull the strawberries and place them in a bowl with the ratafias (or macaroons broken in 3-4 pieces) ; moisten with half the orange juice. Put the grated rind and remaining orange juice in a small basin, add the sugar and stir until dissolved. Whip the cream, sweeten with this orange syrup. Chill both strawberries and orange cream for 1 hour before packing separately in insulated containers. To serve, pile cream on top of fruit.

Prawns sicilienne

6 oz boiled rice (see page 137)
French dressing (see page 137)
paprika pepper
1½ oz almonds (blanched and
    shredded) — see page 134
salt and pepper

For sauce
¼ pint thick mayonnaise (see page
    137)
juice of 1 orange
juice of ½ lemon
1-2 caps of pimiento (sieved)
1 shallot (finely chopped)
2½ fl oz strong fresh tomato pulp
    (see right)
4 oz prawns (shelled)

6-8 dariole moulds

Method

Mix the rice with French dressing (coloured with the paprika)
and add the almonds. Season
well. Put into the dariole moulds
and set aside.

To prepare the sauce : combine the ingredients in the order
given, and adjust seasoning.
Turn out the moulds and spoon
the sauce round the rice.

Watchpoint Soak almonds
(either before or after splitting
and shredding) in warm water
for 30 minutes or longer. This
makes them juicy and tender
and like a fresh nut. Drain well
and dry before adding to rice.

Smoked haddock mousse

8 oz smoked haddock (weighed
    when cooked and flaked — allow
    1 lb on the bone, or ¾ lb fillet)
2 eggs (hard-boiled)
½ pint cold béchamel sauce (see
    page 138)
¼ pint mayonnaise (see page 137)
¼ oz gelatine
2½ fl oz chicken stock (see page 139),
    or water
2½ fl oz double cream (lightly
    whipped)

To finish
2 eggs (hard-boiled)
½-¾ pint aspic jelly (see page 132)

*6-inch diameter top (size No. 2)
    soufflé dish*

Method

Have the haddock ready-
cooked and flaked and the eggs
chopped. Mix the béchamel
sauce and mayonnaise together.
Soak the gelatine in the stock
(or water), dissolve it over
gentle heat and add to the
sauce mixture. Stir in the haddock and eggs and, as the
mixture begins to thicken, fold
in the cream. Turn into the
soufflé dish until about three-
quarters full, cover mousse and
leave it to set in a cool place.

When set, decorate the top
with thin slices of hard-boiled
egg and enough cool aspic to
cover ; leave to set. Fill the dish
with more aspic and leave again
to set before packing the mousse.

Fillet of beef in aspic

1½-2 lb fillet of beef
2-3 tablespoons oil (for roasting)
⅓ pint aspic jelly (this can be made from commercial aspic powder, adding a glass of sherry in place of the same amount of water)

For garnish
4 oz button mushrooms
2 tablespoons olive oil

Method
Roast the fillet at 425°F or Mark 7 for about 35 minutes (see method, page 16). Allow to cool. Wash and trim the mushrooms and slice, if large, but leave whole if quite small. Sauté them in the hot oil for 1 minute only. Tip them on to a plate and allow to cool, then drain on absorbent paper.

Carve the beef, arrange in overlapping slices around a flat serving dish and garnish with the mushrooms. Brush well with cold but still liquid aspic, covering the beef completely.

Tomato pulp
For ½ pint of pulp, take ¾ lb ripe tomatoes (seeds removed) or a 14 oz can. Put in a pan with a clove of garlic (lightly bruised), a bayleaf, salt, and pepper, a slice of onion and a nut of butter. Cover and cock slowly to a thick pulp, about 10-15 minutes. When really thick, pass through a strainer. Adjust seasoning, adding a little sugar if necessary.

Polish potato salad

1½ lb small new potatoes
2 tablespoons white wine
1 small beetroot
1 tablespoon finely grated horseradish
3 tablespoons mayonnaise (see page 137)
½ teaspoon caster sugar
pinch of dry mustard
salt and pepper
2 fl oz plain yoghourt

Method
Cook potatoes in their skins until tender, then skin while still hot and sprinkle with the white wine. Allow to cool.

Grate the beetroot very finely, mix with the horseradish and add to the mayonnaise. Mix sugar, mustard and seasoning together with the yoghourt and add this to the beetroot mixture. Spoon this dressing over the potatoes.

Angel cake Waldorf

2 oz plain flour
6 ½ oz caster sugar
6 egg whites
pinch of salt
¾ teaspoon cream of tarter
3 drops of vanilla essence
2 drops of almond essence

For filling

3-4 oz plain block chocolate
1-2 tablespoons water
½ pint double cream
1 dessertspoon caster sugar

*8-9 inch diameter angel cake tin,
or cake tin with funnelled base*

Method

Set oven at 375°F or Mark 5.

Sift the flour and 3½ oz sugar together 3 times and set aside. Place the egg whites, salt and cream of tartar in a large, perfectly dry basin and whisk with a rotary beater until foamy. Add remaining 3 oz of sugar, 2 tablespoons at a time, and the essences, and continue beating until the mixture will stand in peaks. Carefully fold in the sifted flour and sugar.

Turn the mixture into the clean, dry tin, level the surface and draw a knife through to break any air bubbles. Bake the cake in the pre-set oven for 30-35 minutes or until no imprint remains when a finger lightly touches the top. When the cake is done, turn it upside down on a wire rack and leave until it is quite cold and will fall easily from the tin.

To prepare the filling : melt the chocolate in the water, then allow to cool. Whip the cream until thick, add the sugar and chocolate and continue whisking until it stands in peaks.

Place the cake upside down on a plate or waxed paper. Slice a 1-inch layer off the top of the cake and put this top lid on one side. Cut down and around the inside of the cake 1 inch from the outer edge and 1 inch from the centre hole, leaving a wall of cake about 1 inch thick and a base of 1 inch at the bottom. Remove this middle 'ring' with a spoon (it can be discarded) ; set cake on serving plate. Completely fill the cavity with the chilled filling, replace 'lid' of cake and press gently. Serve a bowl of sugared raspberries or strawberries separately.

Spicy tomato soup

2 lb tomatoes
1 oz butter
2 onions (finely sliced)
1 tablespoon plain flour
1 teaspoon paprika pepper
1 tablespoon tomato purée
3 pints chicken, or turkey, stock (made from giblets) — see page 139

salt and pepper
bouquet garni
1 blade of mace
1 clove
1 oz sago
1 wineglass port

This quantity serves 8 people.

Method
Wipe the tomatoes, cut in half. Squeeze out the seeds and rub them through a nylon strainer to obtain the juice.

Melt the butter in a saucepan, add the sliced onion and cook slowly until soft but not coloured. Blend in the flour, paprika and tomato purée, then add the tomatoes and bruise well with a wooden spoon. Pour on the stock and juice from the tomato seeds, season, add the herbs and spices and stir until boiling. Simmer for 30 minutes, then strain soup.

Return soup to the saucepan with the sago and simmer for about 12 minutes until sago is cooked. Taste for seasoning and finally stir in the port.

Stuffed French loaves

Choose small French loaves (one loaf will serve three hungry people). Cut the top off each loaf, scoop out the crumb and spread the insides very thinly with butter.

Fill each loaf with a 4-egg herb (fines herbes) omelet. Slip the omelets into the loaves straight from the pan and replace the bread tops. Allow omelets to cool, then cut loaves in portions (for easy serving), push tightly together again and wrap in foil.

Herb omelet

4 eggs
1 $\frac{1}{2}$ tablespoons cold water
salt
black pepper (ground from mill)
1 rounded tablespoon mixed chopped herbs (parsley, thyme, marjoram or tarragon, and chives)
1 oz butter

7-8 inch diameter omelet pan

Method
Break the eggs into a basin and beat well with a fork. When well mixed, add water, seasoning and herbs. Heat pan on medium heat, put in butter in two pieces and, when frothing, pour in egg mixture. Leave 10-15 seconds before stirring round slowly with the flat of a fork. Do this once or twice round pan, stop and leave for another 5-6 seconds.

Lift up edge of omelet to let any remaining raw egg run on to hot pan. Tilt the pan away from you and fold over omelet to far side.

67

Stuffed sausages

8 sausages
2 packets Demi-Sel cheese
1 teaspoon French mustard (Dijon)
1 tablespoon tomato pickle, or chutney

Method
Work together all stuffing ingredients until firm. Grill or dry fry your favourite sausages and allow them to cool. Split sausages down one side and fill with the stuffing. Wrap in greaseproof paper or foil and pack in a box.

Lyonnaise salad

4 large potatoes (1-1½ lb)
1 large onion (finely sliced)
2 tablespoons olive oil
4 tablespoons French dressing (see page 137)
1 dill cucumber (sliced)
1 tablespoon chopped parsley

Method
Boil the potatoes in their skins. Meanwhile cook the onion slowly in the oil until it is brown and crisp. Skin and slice potatoes.

Layer potato slices in a salad bowl with the cooked onion. Mix the French dressing with the dill cucumber and parsley and spoon it over the potatoes.

Devilled turkey kebabs

16 pieces of dark turkey meat (cooked)
4½ tablespoons olive oil
¼ teaspoon dry mustard
1 tablespoon Worcestershire sauce
2 tablespoons tomato ketchup, or similar bottled, fruity sauce
dash of Tabasco sauce
1 large green pepper (cored, and deseeded)
12 small mushrooms
4 bayleaves
1 medium-size onion
8 rashers of streaky bacon

8 'lolly' sticks (sharpened at one end)

Method
Mix 1 teaspoon of the oil with the mustard and sauces, pour over turkey meat, and leave to marinate while preparing the other ingredients.

Cut the pepper into squares and blanch in pan of boiling water for 1 minute, then drain and refresh.

Trim the mushroom stalks level with the caps, put into a basin and pour over boiling water, leave for 1 minute, then drain. This preparation of the mushrooms helps to prevent them breaking when they are skewered.

Cut the onion in quarters and divide into segments. Cut each bayleaf in half.

Remove the rind from the bacon and cut each rasher in half, then stretch them by smoothing out with the blade of a heavy knife. Wrap each piece of devilled turkey meat in half a rasher of bacon.

Thread all the ingredients on to the sharpened lolly sticks in the following order : turkey, bayleaf, onion, pepper, mushroom, pepper, turkey.

Brush the finished kebabs with remaining oil and grill until bacon is brown and crisp on all sides. When cold, wrap in greaseproof paper or foil and pack in a box.

1 Cut bacon rashers in half, stretch and wrap round turkey
2 Thread the prepared kebab items on the sharpened sticks
3 Brush with oil and grill until the bacon is brown and crisp. Wrap the kebabs in greaseproof paper or foil

1

2

3

Spanish salad

$\frac{3}{4}$ lb tomatoes
1 large Spanish onion
1 green pepper
salt and pepper
French dressing (made with 2 table-
    spoons white wine and 6 table-
    spoons olive oil — see method,
    page 137)
1 tablespoon mixed chopped herbs
    (parsley, lemon thyme)

Method

Scald, skin and slice the
tomatoes (see page 26). Cut the
onion and pepper in rings,
removing the latter's centre
core and seeds.

Put the onion into pan of cold
water, bring to the boil, then
add the green pepper and boil
for 1 minute ; drain and refresh.

Mix the tomatoes, onion and
pepper together in a salad bowl,
season, spoon over the French
dressing and dust with herbs.

Sticky ginger cake

4 oz butter
4 oz soft brown sugar
2 eggs
10 oz black treacle
8 oz plain flour
pinch of salt
1 teaspoon ground ginger
4 oz sultanas (cleaned)
$\frac{1}{2}$ teaspoon bicarbonate of soda
2 tablespoons warm milk (blood heat)

8-inch diameter cake tin

This cake keeps well and can be
made two weeks before it's
wanted.

Method

Set oven at 325°F or Mark 3.

Grease and flour tin.

Soften the butter in a bowl,
add the sugar and beat
thoroughly until soft ; whisk in
the eggs and black treacle. Sift
the flour with the salt and
ginger and, using a metal spoon,
fold these into the mixture, with
the sultanas.

Dissolve the bicarbonate of
soda in the milk and carefully
stir into cake mixture, pour this
into the prepared tin and bake
in the pre-set oven for $1\frac{1}{2}$-2
hours ; after 1 hour reduce oven
to 300°F or Mark 2.

Cut the cake in wedges,
spread these generously with
unsalted butter and top with
a good slice of Gouda cheese ;
reshape into a cake and wrap
in foil. Serve with crisp apples
(Cox's Orange pippins or
Golden Delicious).

Grant (or granary) loaf

$3\frac{1}{2}$ lb English stone ground
   wholewheat flour
1 dessertspoon salt
1 oz fresh yeast
1 oz sugar (preferably Barbados
   cane sugar)
2 pints 4 fl oz water (at blood heat)

3 loaf tins (2-pints capacity)

This bread, created by Doris Grant, a pioneer in the wholefoods movement, is excellent for sandwiches. Chill briefly before slicing to prevent crumbling. It should keep moist for 5 days as bread and can be used for another few days as toast. Remember that the wholewheat dough must not be kneaded and only requires a few minutes to mix.

Method

Grease the inside of the tins and warm them well.

Mix the salt and flour in a large basin and warm this in the oven or above a low gas flame, so that the yeast will work more quickly.

Crumble the yeast into a large basin, add the sugar and $\frac{1}{4}$ pint of the water. Leave for 10 minutes to froth up, then stir to dissolve the sugar. Pour this yeasty liquid into the basin of warm flour, add the rest of the warm water and stir the whole with a wooden spoon until the flour is evenly wetted. The dough should be so wet that it is slippery — most granary bread is too dry.

Spoon the dough into the warmed tins, put them about 2 feet above a low gas flame (or in the oven while it is warming up to 375°F or Mark 5). Cover with a cloth and leave for about 20 minutes; the dough will rise by about one-third. Then bake in the pre-set oven for 45-60 minutes.

Note : if the bread is not allowed to rise sufficiently before being baked, it will be close in texture, but if allowed to rise too high it will be spongy and not keep moist for so long.

Sandwiches

Bacon and watercress

Take a brown or white sandwich loaf. Cut off the bottom crust, thinly slice the loaf longways, butter two-thirds of the slices and spread remainder on both sides with French mustard.

Grill thin slices of streaky bacon until they are crisp, then leave them to cool. When cool, lay bacon on the buttered slices and cover them with crisp sprigs of watercress. Put the mustard slice in between two of the bacon slices to form a triple sandwich. Lay these on top of each other, with the crust on top.

Set a firm, but not too heavy, weight on top and leave for about 30 minutes before removing the crust and cutting each sandwich into pieces.

Cream cheese and pineapple

Butter the granary bread and cover each slice with a $\frac{1}{2}$-inch layer of cream cheese and cover the bottom slice with chopped watercress. Place a slice of fresh pineapple, cut into bite-size pieces, on top of watercress and top with second slice of bread and cheese.

Prawn

Butter the granary bread and to every $\frac{1}{2}$ pound of prawns take 3 sticks of celery, (chopped), and one sharp dessert apple (peeled, cored and chopped). Bind with 1 tablespoon of tomato chutney and 3 tablespoons of mayonnaise. Mix the prawns into this and fill the buttered bread.

Stuffed rolls

Slice the top off a freshly baked roll and scoop out the crumb. Butter the inside well and season before filling and replacing the top as a lid. Use any of the following fillings :

Coleslaw filling : line the bottom of each roll with a slice of Gruyère or Port Salut cheese, fill with coleslaw and top with a slice of apple before replacing the lid. (To make coleslaw, finely shred raw cabbage, soak well in iced water to crisp, drain and dry throughly before mixing with thick mayonnaise or boiled dressing — see page 137)

Alternatively, fill each roll with coleslaw and put a prune stuffed with chutney or cream cheese and walnut in the middle.

Mango and egg stuffing : coarsely chop hard-boiled eggs and mix to a creamy consistency with béchamel sauce or mayonnaise (see pages 138, 137). Season well, adding 2-3 teaspoons of mango chutney to taste.

Mortadella : soak sliced celery in cold water to crisp ; drain, dry and mix with cream dressing flavoured with horseradish. Line the roll with a slice of mortadella sausage or salami, and fill with the celery mixture. Sliced cheese can be used in place of the sausage.

Fresh fruit jelly

6 clementines
4 ripe dessert pears
1 lb black, or white, grapes
1½ lb lump sugar
3 pints water
finely pared rind and juice of 3
    lemons
4½ oz gelatine (soaked in 14 fl oz
    water)
3 cans (6¼ fl oz each) concentrated
    frozen orange juice (made up with
    2 pints water)

Method
Put the sugar and water in a pan with the lemon rind and juice. Dissolve over gentle heat, then simmer for 5 minutes. Strain this syrup through muslin, wringing it out very well to remove all the syrup and essence from the lemon rind. Add the soaked gelatine to the hot syrup and stir until completely dissolved.
Watchpoint It is important to have the gelatine soaking in the cold water before the sugar syrup is prepared. It should be added to the hot syrup as soon as this has been strained.

Add the diluted orange juice to the sugar syrup and gelatine mixture and allow to cool.

Peel and slice the clementines ; peel, core and slice the ripe pears ; skin and pip the grapes. Arrange the fruit in a polythene container and pour on cool jelly. Cover and allow to set.

Tartlets ricotta

For pastry
1 oz butter
2 oz lard
6 oz plain flour
pinch of salt
about 3 tablespoons water

For filling
10 oz curd cheese (home-made),
    or Demi-Sel
salt and pepper
3 eggs
2-3 oz smoked salmon, or ham
1-2 oz Gruyère cheese

12-16 tartlet tins, or 7-8 inch diameter flan ring

Method
Set oven at 375-400°F or Mark 5-6.

Rub the fats into the flour and salt and mix with the water to a firm dough.

To prepare filling : sieve and cream the curd cheese and add the seasoning. Beat the eggs and gradually add them to the cheese. Cut the salmon (or ham) into shreds and mix carefully into the egg and cheese mixture.

Roll out the pastry and line on to tarlet tins or flan ring. Fill with the prepared mixture. Cut the Gruyère cheese into thin slices and lay these over the top. Bake in the pre-set oven until golden-brown and crisp, about 12-15 minutes for tartlets, or about 25 minutes for a flan.

Barbecue equipment

The equipment available today means that outdoor cooking no longer demands the skill to make a hunter's fire (built in a hollow between two logs, end-open to the wind), or any other type of camp fire. A pity, since there is no substitute for experience when it comes to barbecue cooking, and people who have cooked on camp fires have learnt the hard way that you don't cook satisfactorily on briskly burning fuel — you have to let your fire burn down until all that is left is a bed of red-hot embers.

Equipment for outdoor cooking ranges from simple portable barbecues costing under £ 2 to elaborate barbecue trolleys.

Almost any sort of meat or fish can be grilled outdoors, direct on the bars of the grill, on skewers or a griddle, in a frying pan, or in little parcels of foil. A dish that tastes delicious grilled over charcoal is lamb loin chops (known in French as carré d'agneau), see page 81.

In general, meat and fish grilled over a fire need to be basted frequently or they will dry out. Since falling fat splutters on the fire in a barbecue and makes it flame, the baste is usually a sauce.

Barbecue meals do not need a lot of expensive equipment, although the paraphernalia is part of the fun. Tongs or gloves for handling the food, a long-handled spoon or paint brush for basting, a bulb syringe filled with water to damp down flames from dripping fat are a great help.

1 *Simplest, do-it-yourself barbecue. Ordinary bricks, in two rows of five, form a base for the charcoal ; eight more bricks give protection from the wind. An oven shelf or grill tray laid across holds food at the right height over the embers. Hardly portable, but size is adjustable*

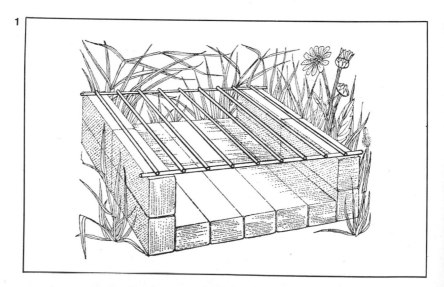

Home-made barbecue

A simple, inexpensive and effective barbecue can be built from about 18 bricks, preferably laid on bare earth, concrete or stone. Put the bricks together flat on the ground in two rows of five. Then build up two opposite ends, each with four bricks placed on their sides. This structure will support an ordinary oven shelf or metal bars which can then be used as a grill (see illustration opposite).

The fuel to use is charcoal, which can be bought or ordered from most ironmongers in convenient 14 lb bags. Lay the fire in the usual way with newspaper, small dry sticks and then charcoal. Solid fuel tablets, in packets of 20, are obtainable from chemists and are a great help in starting a fire. (Firelighters are inclined to leave a rather unpleasant lingering paraffin smell.)

If there is a great deal of draught, block up the third side of the barbecue with four more bricks until the charcoal is well and truly alight, then remove them. Keep the fire fairly flat over the surface of the bricks — a bed of embers, about 3 inches thick, is what most people find right for grilling — putting on more charcoal as necessary with a pair of tongs. Don't begin cooking until the charcoal glows, which will take about 30-40 minutes.

2 *Le Creuset charcoal-burning BarbeKit has four legs, four sides, a base, a grill and a pair of lifting tongs, packed in a neat wooden box with carrying handle. Assembled in seconds, it measures $8\frac{1}{2}$ inches square by 8 inches high, and a number of kits can be fitted together. Its cast-iron construction stands up to wear, and it's portable enough for a picnic*

Barbecue equipment continued

3

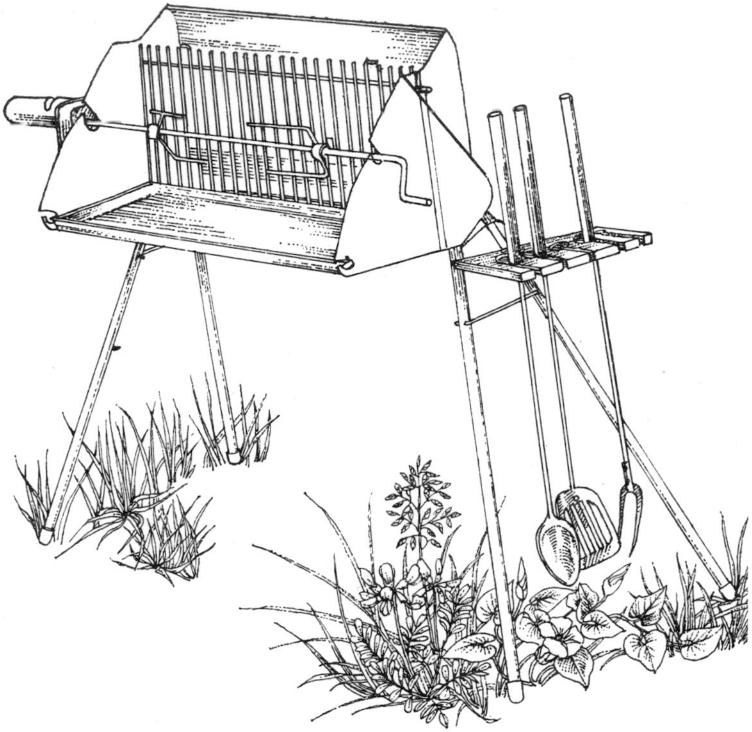

4

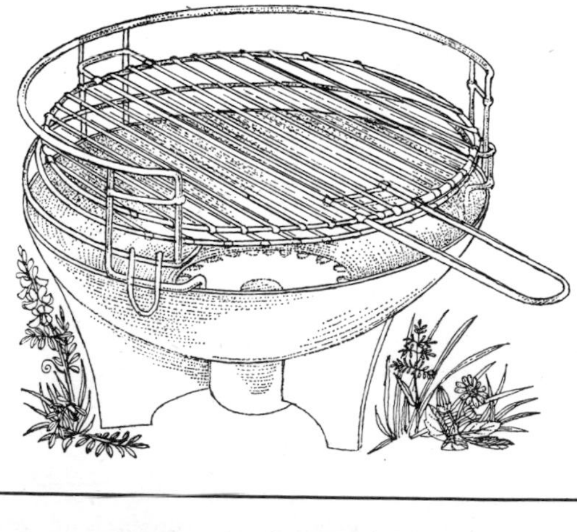

3 *Le Creuset Super Convertible barbecue can be changed from grill to roast position in 3 seconds. It has a powerful battery-operated spit roaster, a stainless steel basting tray, and comes complete with barbecue tools. Measures 18 inches by 10 inches by 2½ feet high, and folds flat into a box 2 feet 3½ inches by 11 inches by 6½ inches high*

4 *Le Creuset charcoal-burning, cast-iron Hibachi barbecue stove is dual purpose. It can be used indoors in a chimney or on a balcony, or outdoors, and is ideal for kebabs. Has a quick lighting system, three heating positions and a double grill. Height is variable, ranging approximately from 7-9 inches, and it's 12 inches in diameter*

Buying equipment

When you come to buy barbecue equipment, the best choice in Great Britain is, in fact, limited to comparatively few large stores. Most of the more elaborate equipment is imported, home-produced types being inexpensive and simple, consisting usually of a metal fire box on legs, with a grill, and provision for a hand-turned spit.

The grill should be capable of being fixed in a least two positions to give different heats, and there should be a windshield. After that, the choice is entirely a matter of individual taste and pocket ; however, it is worth paying for cast-iron fire boxes, and for easy assembly, if a portable barbecue is what you want. Rectangular barbecues give more useful space than round ones.

Some barbecues have battery-operated spits, and they are also made to operate off bottled gas, but, of course, this involves 'griddle' cooking, not searing over glowing charcoal, which imparts its own subtle flavour to the food being cooked. However, solid griddles are useful for outdoor cooking and can be bought separately and used over the grill bars, when needed, on bottled gas and charcoal versions.

Brochettes of kidney

Allow one skewer per person and for each skewer the following ingredients :

2 lambs kidneys
2 or 3 squares of lambs liver
boiled rice (for serving)
chopped parsley (to garnish)

For marinade
2 ½ fl oz olive oil
2-3 tablespoons red wine
few sprigs of thyme
salt
pepper (ground from mill)

Method

Skin and split kidneys, cut the liver into 1-1$\frac{1}{2}$ inch squares and remove the ducts. Marinate the liver and kidneys in the mixture of oil and red wine, adding seasoning and the thyme. Leave for 2-3 hours.

Thread the kidneys and liver alternately on to skewers and grill for 6-8 minutes, moistening with the marinade throughout the cooking time.

Serve brochettes on a bed of boiled rice and sprinkle with chopped parsley. Serve with bowl of crisp bacon rolls.

Bacon rolls

Allow 2 rashers of finely cut streaky bacon per person. Remove the rind and rust. Stroke out rashers with blunt blade of a heavy knife until really thin. Cut them in half, then spread with French mustard. Roll up and skewer. These rolls can be grilled or baked, but they must be crisp and brown.

Below left : cutting liver into squares and marinating the skinned and split kidneys for the brochettes
Below : threading the liver and kidney on to skewers (see photograph of the finished dish opposite)

Barbecued lamb chops

2 neck, or loin, lamb chops per person
oil

For barbecue sauce
2 large cooking apples (peeled and cored)
1 medium-size onion
¼ pint tomato ketchup
2 tablespoons brown sugar
½ teaspoon salt
¼ teaspoon black pepper
2 oz butter

Method

Brush chops with oil and leave for 1-2 hours before cooking.

To prepare the sauce : grate or mince the apple and onion into a saucepan, add all the other ingredients and bring to boil ; simmer for 2-3 minutes. Grill lamb chops for 3 minutes on each side, spoon a little of the barbecue sauce over them and continue cooking a further 3 minutes until sauce is brown and sticky. Serve very hot with the remaining barbecue sauce handed separately and a spicy potato salad (see page 84) in a separate dish.

Devilled poussins

2 double poussins
2 oz butter
watercress (to garnish)

For dry devil mixture
1 dessertspoon salt
1 dessertspoon caster sugar
1 teaspoon ground pepper
1 teaspoon ground ginger
1 teaspoon dry mustard
½ teaspoon curry powder
2 tablespoons tomato chutney
1 tablespoon mushroom ketchup
1 tablespoon Worcestershire sauce
1 tablespoon soy sauce
1 tablespoon fruit sauce such as plum, gooseberry, or A.1
dash of Tabasco sauce
stock, or potato water

Method

Split the poussins in half and cut away the back and rib bones. Mix the dry devil ingredients together and rub well into the surface of the birds. Leave them for at least 1 hour.

Melt the butter in a small saucepan. Brush the poussins with plenty of the melted butter and grill them slowly until brown and crisp, about 10 minutes each side. Then remove the grid from the grill pan and place the birds at the bottom.

Mix all the sauces together in the pan with the remaining butter, heat gently and then spoon over the poussins. Continue cooking (for about 5-7 minutes), basting continually with the sauce.

Take up the poussins, arrange in a serving dish, dilute the sauce in the pan with a little stock (or potato water) and spoon it over the top. Garnish with watercress and serve Simla rice (see page 84) separately.

Carré d'agneau (see cover photograph)

best end of neck of lamb (about 1½ lb)
pepper (ground from the mill)
chopped rosemary, or thyme

1

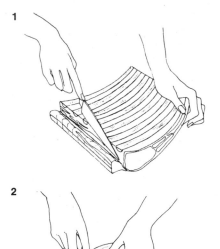

Method
Ask the butcher to chine the lamb. Start preparing the joint by removing the chine bone completely (see diagram 1). This can be used for gravy.

With a sharp knife, cut through the flesh about 3 inches from the end of the cutlet bones (diagram 2). Remove the fat and meat, scraping the bones clean (diagram 3), with the knife.

2

Sprinkle with fresh black pepper ground from the mill and chopped rosemary, or thyme.

Grill for about 35-40 minutes, turning frequently to prevent burning. There should be sufficient fat on the joint to keep it moist without adding any extra.

Carve by slicing down alongside each bone.

3

STEAK CUTS

Rump ($1\frac{1}{2}$ lb slice, 1 inch thick, serves 3-4)
This steak has incomparable flavour but to be tender must be
well hung. A guide to this is the colour, which should have a
purplish tinge with creamy-white fat. It improves if brushed
with oil 1-2 hours before grilling. During grilling time
brush once or twice with oil to prevent scorching

Sirloin or entrecôte ($\frac{3}{4}$-1 inch thick, serves 1)
This steak is cut from the top part of the sirloin

Minute ($\frac{1}{2}$ inch thick, serves 1)
Thin slice of entrecôte. This steak should be cooked very
rapidly and to get it properly browned without over-cooking,
dry fry rather than grill

T-Bone (1 $\frac{1}{2}$-2 inches thick, serves 2-3)
A whole slice cut from the sirloin with the bone

Porterhouse (1 $\frac{1}{2}$-2 inches thick, serves 1-2)
A slice cut from the wing rib, taken off the bone

Fillet (1-1$\frac{1}{2}$ inches thick, serves 1)
The most expensive and possibly most tender of steaks.
There is a large demand for these slices cut across the fillet,
so they are in short supply. The fillet (averaging 6-7 lb) lies
under the sirloin and there is a comparatively small proportion
of fillet in relation to the weight of the rest of the animal.
Dry fry or grill

Tournedos (1-1$\frac{1}{2}$ inches thick, serves 1)
These are cut from the 'eye' of the fillet, ie. from centre after
it has been trimmed (fillet steaks include the side or edges,
ie. trimmings). A tournedos is very much a delicacy and may
be served plainly grilled or dry fried with a garnish as for a
fillet steak, or as a dish such as tournedos chasseur. The
crisp dry fat in which fillet is encased (kidney suet) is very
special ; a small nut of this may be fried or grilled to top each
tournedos

Chateaubriand (3-4 inches thick, serves 2)
A thick cut taken from the heart of the fillet. This steak, once
grilled or dry fried, is sliced downwards for serving

GRILLING TIMES

Rare :	6-7 minutes
Medium rare :	8-10 minutes
Well done :	14-16 minutes

Rare :	5 minutes
Medium rare :	6-7 minutes
Well done :	9-10 minutes

Rare :	1-1½ minutes
Medium rare :	2-3 minutes

Rare :	7-8 minutes
Medium rare :	8-10 minutes

Rare :	7-8 minutes
Medium rare :	8-10 minutes

Rare :	6 minutes
Medium rare to well done	7-8 minutes

Rare :	6 minutes
Medium rare to well done :	7-8 minutes

Rare to medium rare :	16-20 minutes

Salad accompaniments

Mixed vegetable salad

1 **hard white Dutch cabbage (weighing 3 lb)**
1 **lb carrots**
1 **head of celery**
6 **tablespoons olive oil**
salt
pepper (ground from mill)
4 **crisp dessert apples**
3 **tablespoons white wine vinegar**
2½ **fl oz soured, or fresh, cream**

Method

Shred cabbage very finely and soak in ice-cold water while preparing the other ingredients.

Peel and grate carrots. Wash celery and cut in julienne strips.

Drain cabbage and place it in a large bowl ; add oil and mix thoroughly until every shred is well coated, then add seasoning to taste.

Peel, core and slice the apples and mix with the cabbage. Add the carrot and celery and wine vinegar and cream and mix until thoroughly blended. Adjust the seasoning and serve salad in large bowls.

Adding apples to the shredded cabbage after tossing it in oil

83

Salad accompaniments continued

Spicy potato salad

6 lb even-size old potatoes
½ lb streaky bacon
2 tablespoons malt vinegar
English mustard (dry)
1 jar of green pepper relish
¾ pint mayonnaise (see page 137)
1 tablespoon celery seed

Method
Boil the potatoes in their skins until tender, then peel while hot. Meanwhile, fry the bacon until brown and crisp, remove it from the pan with a draining spoon, put in a bowl and crumble with a fork. Take the frying pan off the heat, add the vinegar, then pour off liquid into a small basin.

Thinly slice enough potato to make a layer in the serving dish, sprinkle with a ¼ teaspoon of the mustard and 1 tablespoon of the relish, then cover with a layer of crumbled bacon with a little of the bacon fat, followed by a layer of mayonnaise and a sprinkling of celery seeds. Continue layering the potatoes in this way and finish with mayonnaise.

Simla rice

6 oz long grain rice
1½-2 oz butter
1 medium-size onion (finely sliced)
about 1 teaspoon turmeric
salt and pepper

Method
Cook the rice in plenty of boiling salted water until tender (about 12 minutes). Turn it into a colander and refresh with a jug

of hot water. Allow it to drain thoroughly.

Melt the butter, add the onion and cook slowly until golden-brown, stir in the turmeric, allow it to cook for about 2 minutes, then fork in the rice. Toss over the heat and season to taste.

Les crudités

carrots
beetroot
swedes (preferably Cornish)
cabbage (drumhead, or Dutch)
celery
about ½ pint French dressing (see page 137)
1 bunch of watercress

Method
Prepare the salad 1 hour before serving. Grate the carrot, beetroot and swedes separately on a fine grater and put each vegetable into separate bowls. Finely shred the cabbage and celery separately and put into separate bowls. Moisten each vegetable with French dressing and carefully arrange each kind in sections in a large wooden or china salad bowl.

Set a bunch of watercress in the centre and serve the salad with hot rolls. Hand a bowl of boiled dressing separately (see page 137)

Socials and summer buffets

How do you cater for more people than you have chairs ? How do you feed people who all arrive at different times ? The answer is to provide a buffet, and from an array of tempting dishes, guests can choose to suit their own appetites. Many of the dishes will of course be cold, but not all. Use a heated tray if you have one, or bring out hot foods fresh from the oven from time to time.

Cold Shannon soup

4 cans (7½ fl oz each) concentrated
beef consommé
1 can (11½ oz) vegetable juice
1 can (11½ oz) tomato juice
dash of Tabasco sauce
¼ pint double cream

For serving
2 lemons
extra double cream (lightly
whipped) — optional
grated nutmeg (optional)

Store cans in refrigerator for 12
hours before making the soup.
This quantity serves 12 people.

Method
Turn the consommé into a large
mixing bowl, add the vegetable
and tomato juices and Tabasco
and whisk together until
thoroughly blended. Then stir
in the cream and pour into
small soup cups. Return to the
refrigerator to chill again. The
soup should be just set.
    Serve each with a wedge of
lemon. If wished, add 1 teaspoon of lightly whipped cream
and dust with a little nutmeg.

Spiced ham and egg salad

12 eggs (hard-boiled)
1 lb sliced ham
1 teaspoon paprika pepper
salt and pepper
dash of Tabasco sauce
2 tablespoons red wine vinegar
4 tablespoons tomato ketchup
6 tablespoons salad oil
3 tablespoons mango chutney
1 pinch of saffron (soaked in 2
tablespoons boiling water for
about 30 minutes)
½ pint mayonnaise (see page 137)
1 lb long grain rice (boiled, drained
and dried well) — see page 137
watercress (to garnish)

This quantity serves 12 people.

Method
Mix the paprika, salt and pepper
and Tabasco with the vinegar
and stir in the tomato ketchup.
Then add the oil, whisk well
until the mixture thickens and
taste for seasoning. If the mango
chutney is rather coarse, cut
the mango into thin strips ; add
to the dressing. Cut the ham
into shreds and mix with the
dressing.
    Strain the saffron through a
nylon strainer and beat into
the mayonnaise. Taste the
mayonnaise for seasoning and
then mix into the rice. Arrange
this rice on a serving dish. Cut
the hard-boiled eggs in half
and arrange on top of the rice.
Spoon the spiced ham mixture
over the eggs and garnish
the dish with watercress.

Gooseberry cream

3 lb gooseberries
1½ pints water
9 tablespoons granulated sugar
3 oz gelatine
1½ pints double cream
4½ tablespoons caster sugar
8-9 drops edible green colouring

For decoration
3 pints lemon jelly (see page 133)
pistachio nuts, or small
  diamonds of angelica

*Three 6-7 inch diameter cake tins,
  or charlotte tins*

This quantity serves 12 people.

Method
Top and tail the gooseberries and poach them until tender in a syrup made from the water and granulated sugar ; then drain and rub fruit through a nylon sieve. Set this purée and 1½ pints of the syrup on one side.

Line the moulds with the cold but still liquid jelly, decorate the bottom with pistachio nuts (or angelica), setting the decoration in sufficient jelly to cover.

Add half of the reserved syrup to the gelatine, allow it to soak and then dissolve it over gentle heat. Half whip the cream in a bowl, add the fruit purée, remaining syrup, sugar and colouring. Add the melted gelatine, stir gently with the bowl set on ice cubes until cream begins to thicken, then pour it at once into the prepared moulds. Leave it in the refrigerator or a cool place to set firm.

Smoked haddock quiche

For shortcrust pastry
1 lb plain flour
pinch of salt
8 oz shortening
4 oz butter
about 6-8 tablespoons water (to mix)

For filling
1 lb smoked haddock fillet
   (cooked and flaked)
2 oz streaky bacon rashers
1 oz butter
2 eggs
2 egg yolks
2 oz grated Cheddar cheese
¼ pint milk
¼ pint single cream
pepper (ground from mill)
salt (optional)

Two 8-inch diameter flan rings

This quantity serves 8 people.

Method
First make the pastry (see method, page 136) and chill for about 15 minutes. Then roll out and line flan rings. Set oven at 375°F or Mark 5.

Remove the rind from the bacon and cut into thin strips. Cook in a pan with the butter until frizzled. Beat the whole eggs and yolks with the cheese and milk in a bowl ; pour this over the cooked flaked haddock and add the bacon and cream. Season with a little pepper, but taste the mixture before adding any salt as it is quite possible that the haddock, cheese and bacon will make the filling salty enough.

Put mixture in the pastry-lined flan rings and bake in pre-set oven until the filling is set and the top is golden-brown (about 25 minutes).

Watchpoint As this filling is made with egg it is important that the oven is not too hot. To make sure that the pastry is well baked on the underside, place a baking sheet in the oven while pre-heating and then place the flans on top for baking ; this will give extra bottom heat.

Serve salads in separate bowls.

Tunny fish and egg salad

2 cans (7½ oz each) tunny fish
4 eggs (hard-boiled)
2 lb tomatoes
1½ cucumbers (peeled)
salt
1 lb frozen French, or sliced,
   beans
1 small can anchovy fillets
1 tablespoon mixed chopped herbs
   (½ parsley, ¼ mint and ¼ chives)
French dressing (made from 2 tablespoons white wine vinegar, salt
   and pepper, 6 tablespoons salad
   oil — see method page 137)
12 black olives (halved and stoned)

Large gratin dish

If no fresh herbs are available,
use ½ tablespoon dried basil
and oregano (mixed). This
quantity serves 8 people.

Method

Scald and skin the tomatoes ;
cut ½ lb into quarters and the
remainder in thick slices. Slice
the half cucumber very finely,
salt it and keep between 2
plates. Cut the other cucumber
in thicker slices, or into small
cubes, and sprinkle with salt.
Cook the beans in boiling water
until tender and then drain and
refresh. Drain the anchovy fillets
from the oil and each fillet
in half lengthways.

Flake the tunny fish and slice
the hard-boiled eggs. Layer the
sliced tomatoes, beans and
thickly cut cucumber (drained
of the water), tunny fish and
hard-boiled eggs in a large
gratin dish. Add the herbs to
the French dressing, whisk well
and spoon over the salad.
Place the thinly cut cucumber,
also drained of water, over the
top of the salad. Arrange the
anchovy fillets in a lattice over
the top of the cucumber and
place a half olive in each
square. Arrange the quartered
tomatoes around the outside
of the dish.

Serve with potatoes baked in
their jackets.

Spaghetti and ham au gratin

1 lb spaghetti
8 oz ham, or pork luncheon meat
(cut in dice, or julienne strips)
4 tablespoons tomato chutney
1½ oz butter
1 oz plain flour
1 dessertspoon English mustard
(mixed to a paste with cold water)
½ pint water
½ pint milk
salt and pepper
3 eggs (beaten)
2 oz grated Cheddar cheese

2 pie dishes (1½ -2 pints capacity)

This dish can be prepared in advance and baked just before serving. This quantity serves 8 people.

Method

Cook the spaghetti in plenty of boiling salted water until tender (12-15 minutes). Drain, refresh with a jug of hot water and drain again. Return the spaghetti to the saucepan and cover with warm water while preparing the other ingredients.

Butter the pie dishes and set oven at 375°F or Mark 5. Mix the ham (or pork luncheon meat) with the tomato chutney and keep on one side.

Melt the butter in a pan, blend in the flour and cook very gently until straw-coloured and marbled in appearance. Blend in the made mustard, water and milk. Season and stir until boiling. Tip mixture into a bowl and allow to cool. Then add the beaten eggs. Drain the spaghetti again and mix in the mustard sauce ; turn into buttered pie dishes, layering it with the ham mixture. Cover the top with the grated cheese and bake in the pre-set oven until set and brown on the top (about 30 minutes).

Serve salads in separate bowls.

Lemon sponge

rind and juice of 4 lemons
1 oz gelatine
4 oz caster sugar
1 pint water
4 egg whites
2 tablespoons sherry

For decoration
6-8 fl oz double cream
(whipped)
few glacé cherries
little angelica (optional)

This quantity serves 6-8 people.

Method
Pare the rind of the lemons very finely with a potato peeler. Put rind in a saucepan with the gelatine, sugar and water and dissolve very slowly over gentle heat. Strain into a basin and allow to cool.

Strain the lemon juice, add to the cooled mixture with the egg whites and sherry and whisk together until white and frothy. Pour into a glass dish and leave until set. Decorate with the cream, glacé cherries, and angelica, if wished.

Coffee jelly

2 pints strong black coffee (made with ground coffee beans, or freeze-dried instant coffee)
2 oz gelatine
¼ pint water
4 oz granulated sugar
thinly pared rind of 1 orange

For decoration
5 fl oz double, or whipping, cream (whipped, sweetened and flavoured with vanilla essence)
1 oz flaked browned almonds (see page 134)

This quantity serves 8 people.

Method
Melt the gelatine in the water. Add the sugar and orange rind to the freshly made coffee and stir gently until the sugar is dissolved, then cover and leave to infuse for 10 minutes. Strain coffee through a double thickness of muslin, add the gelatine mixture and pour into two glass bowls. Leave to set.

Cover with the flavoured cream and scatter over the browned almonds.

Avocado mousse

2-3 avocado pears (to give ¾ pint pulp)
½ oz gelatine
scant ¼ pint cold water
scant ¼ pint boiling water, or chicken stock (see page 139)
1 teaspoon salt
1 teaspoon onion juice (from finely grated onion)
2 teaspoons Worcestershire sauce
¼ pint mayonnaise (see page 137)
¼ pint double cream (lightly whipped)

For garnish
2 green peppers
1-2 oz black olives
2 tablespoons French dressing (see page 137)

Ring mould (1½ pints capacity)

This quantity serves 6-8 people.

Method

Oil the ring mould. Soak the gelatine in the cold water for 5 minutes, then tip on the boiling water (or stock) and stir until dissolved. Peel and quarter the avocados, removing the stones, crush with a fork ; add gelatine liquid with salt, onion juice and Worcestershire sauce. When mixture is cold, fold in the mayonnaise and cream. Pour the mousse into the oiled mould and leave in a cool place to set.

Meanwhile, prepare the garnish. Shred the peppers, removing the core and all the seeds, then blanch them in boiling water for 1 minute ; drain and refresh with cold water. Halve and stone the black olives. Mix the French dressing with the peppers and black olives.

Turn out the mousse and fill the centre with the green pepper and olive salad.

Serve a savoury mousse as a starter for a buffet lunch party

Eggs Indochine

8 eggs (hard-boiled)
4 oz butter (well creamed)
1 teaspoon tomato purée

For salad
1 cucumber
1 teaspoon salt
1 tablespoon olive oil
½ teaspoon caster sugar
pepper (ground from mill)
1 teaspoon white wine vinegar
½ lb prawns (shelled)
1 teaspoon chopped parsley,
   or mint

For curry cream dressing
1 tablespoon chopped onion
1 clove of garlic (chopped)
2 tablespoons oil
1 dessertspoon curry powder
¼ pint tomato juice
1 slice of lemon
1 tablespoon apricot jam
½ pint mayonnaise (see page 137)
extra lemon juice (for mayonnaise)
   —optional
extra salt and pepper (for
   mayonnaise) — optional

This quantity serves 6-8 people.

Method

First prepare the curry cream dressing : cook the onion and garlic in the oil until soft but not coloured, add the curry powder and continue cooking for 1 minute. Pour on the tomato juice, add the lemon and cook gently for 7-10 minutes. Stir in the apricot jam and boil up well. Strain dressing and leave to cool.

To prepare the salad : cut the cucumber into julienne strips, sprinkle with the salt, cover and leave in a cool place for about 30 minutes. Drain away liquid and wipe away any visible salt with absorbent paper. Turn cucumber gently in the oil until completely covered. Season with sugar and pepper, sprinkle on the vinegar and mix again. Mix the prawns and parsley (or mint) with the cucumber.

Halve the eggs, take out the yolks and rub them through a wire strainer ; mix these with the butter, tomato purée and about 1 teaspoon of the curry mixture. Wash and dry the egg whites, fill with the mixture, and reshape. Dish up the eggs in a semi-circle on a serving dish. Add the remaining curry dressing to the mayonnaise with extra seasoning and lemon juice added, if necessary. Use about half this sauce to coat the eggs.

Pile the salad in the centre of the dish. Serve the remaining sauce in a bowl or sauce boat.

Cutting the cucumber into julienne strips for salad to accompany eggs

Fillet of beef niçoise

1½ lb fillet of beef
2-3 tablespoons olive oil (for
   roasting)
1 pint aspic jelly (see page 132)

For salad
1 large aubergine
4 tablespoons olive oil
1 onion (sliced)
2 green peppers (cored, shredded
   and blanched)
salt and pepper
1 lb tomatoes (skinned, quartered
   and seeds removed — see page
   26)
2-3 tablespoons French dressing
   (see page 137)

For garnish
3 eggs (hard-boiled and quartered,
   or sliced)
2 oz black olives (stoned)

For cream dressing
1 clove of garlic (crushed with a
   little salt)
1 teaspoon paprika pepper
1 large carton of soured, or
   cultured, cream
pepper (ground from mill)
lemon juice, or wine vinegar
   (to taste)

This quantity serves 6-8 people.

Method
Roast the fillet of beef in the oven at 400°F or Mark 7 for about 35 minutes and then leave to cool (see method, page 16).

Meanwhile, prepare the salad. Slice the aubergine, score the cut surface with a knife, sprinkle with salt and leave it for 20-30 minutes, then drain away the liquid.

Heat the oil in a frying pan and lightly fry aubergine slices on both sides. Reduce the heat, add the onion to the pan and continue cooking until it is soft but not coloured, then add the peppers and seasoning and cook for 2-3 minutes when the aubergine should be tender. Increase the heat under the pan, add the tomatoes and cook briskly for 1 minute. Turn the salad into a dish and leave to cool, then moisten with French dressing.

To prepare the cream dressing: work the crushed garlic and paprika into the soured (or cultured) cream. Season with pepper and add the lemon juice (or wine vinegar) to taste.

Carve the beef, arrange in overlapping slices round a flat serving dish. Brush well with cool aspic jelly, giving 2-3 coats, and leave to set. Spoon salad into centre of dish and garnish with eggs and olives. Serve dressing and hot anchovy loaf separately.

Frying the aubergine and onion slices in oil on both sides before adding the peppers and tomatoes

Basting the cold slices of roast beef with 2-3 coats of cool aspic jelly, allowing each coat to set before adding the next

Hot anchovy loaf

French loaf
6 anchovy fillets (soaked in a little milk)
3-4 oz unsalted butter
anchovy essence
pepper

Method
Drain anchovy fillets and chop. Pound with the butter and add enough anchovy essence to flavour well and colour the butter a delicate pink. Season with pepper.

Slice the French loaf evenly down to the crust, but not right through. Spread anchovy butter between slices and on top and sides of loaf. Wrap in foil and bake in oven until crisp and golden-brown (about 20 minutes).

Chicken salad milanaise

3-4 lb roasting chicken
2 oz butter
pinch of marjoram
salt and pepper
1 wineglass dry vermouth
$\frac{1}{2}$ pint jellied chicken stock (see page 139)
4 oz cooked ham
4 oz cooked tongue

For salad
8 oz cut macaroni
$\frac{1}{2}$ lb button mushrooms (washed and trimmed)
juice of $\frac{1}{4}$ lemon
2 tablespoons olive oil
salt and pepper
$\frac{1}{4}$ pint mayonnaise (see page 137)

For garnish
1 bunch of watercress

This quantity serves 10-12 people.

Method
Set the oven at 400°F or Mark 6.

Put $\frac{1}{2}$ oz of the butter, the marjoram and seasoning inside the chicken, truss bird neatly and rub the remaining butter over it. Place bird in a roasting tin, pour round vermouth, cover breast with a buttered paper and put in the pre-set oven. Baste bird after 20 minutes, remove paper and turn chicken on its side ; continue to baste it every 20 minutes. When the vermouth has evaporated and the butter begins to brown, add a little of the jellied stock. Turn the bird as it browns and finish the cooking with the breast uppermost. (Total cooking time, about 1-1$\frac{1}{2}$ hours.)

Remove the bird from the roasting tin and leave to cool. Tip the remaining stock into the roasting tin, bring to the boil and scrape down sediment from the sides of the pan. Strain this and leave to cool.

To prepare the salad : cook the macaroni in boiling salted water until just tender (about 12-15 minutes), drain and rinse under the cold tap until very shiny. Cut the mushrooms in thick slices, put in a pan with the lemon juice and cook very quickly for 1 minute only, turn out on to a plate to cool. Sprinkle the mushrooms with the oil, turning them in it carefully until completely coated, then season. Mix the mayonnaise into the macaroni, add the mushrooms and turn the salad carefully into the serving dish. Carve the chicken, cutting the flesh in neat, even-size pieces (removing the bones) and arrange on top of the salad.

Cut the ham and tongue into julienne strips. Remove all traces of fat from the cooking liquor from the chicken (this is easy if it is cold) and mix the remainder with the strips of ham and tongue.

Watchpoint Ham soon loses its pink colour if exposed to the air, so if you shred the ham and tongue in advance keep meat in a small basin covered with a piece of wet greaseproof paper.

Spoon the ham and tongue over the chicken and garnish with the watercress.

Gâteau Margot

4 oz plain flour
4 eggs
6 oz caster sugar
pinch of salt

For filling
1 lb strawberries (or 2 packets of frozen ones)
1 tablespoon caster sugar
4 oz plain block chocolate
½ pint double cream
vanilla essence

Ring mould (3 pints capacity)

This quantity serves 12 people.

Method

Set oven at 375°F or Mark 5. Grease, sugar and flour the tin or mould. Sift the flour with the salt and set aside. Whisk the eggs and sugar together over hot water until thick and mousse-like (no heat is necessary if an electric mixer is used). Remove the bowl from the heat and continue beating until the mixture is cold ; fold in flour with a metal spoon and turn at once into the prepared tin. Bake in the pre-set oven for about 35-40 minutes ; cool on a rack.

Meanwhile, take about one-third of the strawberries, cut in thick slices, sprinkle with caster sugar and leave for 10-15 minutes, then rub them through a nylon strainer to make a purée. Grate the chocolate on to a plate ; place over a pan of hot water to melt.

Cut the cake across in three rounds, spread the two lower layers with a thin coating of chocolate and leave to set. Whip the cream until thick, take about one-third and flavour with the strawberry purée.

Spread this over the chocolate-covered layers and sandwich the whole cake together. Sweeten and flavour the remaining cream with vanilla and spread over the cake with a palette knife. Pile remaining strawberries in middle.

Spiced beef 1

5 lb silverside of beef
meat glaze (for brushing) — optional

For spice mixture
2 cloves of garlic
3 oz soft brown sugar
1 oz saltpetre
1 oz allspice (crushed or pounded)
2 bayleaves (chopped or powdered)
4 oz salt

For cooking
2 onions (quartered)
2 carrots (quartered)
1 stick of celery (sliced)
large bouquet garni
cold water

Piece of butter muslin

This quantity serves 10 people.

Method

Peel garlic and split each clove into 3-4 pieces, make small incisions in the meat with the point of a knife and insert pieces of garlic. Mix other spice ingredients together in a bowl and rub well over meat (saltpetre gives meat a pinkish colour). Keep in a deep dish in a cool larder or refrigerator for a week, rub meat well every day with spice mixture.

Then take out meat, tie it in muslin and put into a large pan with the prepared vegetables and bouquet garni. Cover well with cold water, put lid on the pan and simmer for 3-4 hours until meat is tender.

Cool slightly in the liquid, then take out meat, remove muslin, and set meat in a deep dish with an enamel plate on top of it with at least a 4 lb (or equivalent) weight on it. Leave overnight. Serve plain or brushed with meat glaze.

To make meat glaze boil down a little brown stock until it is thick and syrupy and brown in colour. Cool a little before use.

Spiced beef 2

4-5 lb salted brisket of beef
10 peppercorns
large bouquet garni
2 onions (quartered)
2 carrots (quartered)
1 stick of celery (cut in four)
cold water

This quantity serves 8-10 people.

Method

Cut beef in two and put in a large pan. Add peppercorns, the bouquet garni, prepared vegetables and water to cover. Simmer until meat is tender (about 3-4 hours), then lift out into a deep dish.

Put one piece of beef on top of the other and run a short thin skewer vertically through each end, pressing them down to level with top of meat.

Put an enamel plate on top of meat with at least a 4 lb (or equivalent) weight on it. Leave overnight. Remove plate and weight. Brush with 2-3 coats of meat glaze (see left).

Dressing for brawn or rich meats

Put 4 rounded tablespoons of brown sugar, 6 tablespoons of wine vinegar, $\frac{1}{4}$ pint of salad oil, 1 tablespoon of ready-made English mustard, and some salt and black pepper into a screw-top jar. Shake this vigorously until it is well blended. Taste and adjust seasoning. This dressing will keep up to 2 weeks in a cool place.

Pork brawn

$\frac{1}{2}$ pig's head (salted)
1-1$\frac{1}{2}$ lb shin of beef
1 large onion (peeled)
large bouquet garni
cold water
black pepper (ground from mill)

Two 7-inch diameter basins

This quantity serves 10-12 people. It is difficult to cut down on the quantity given above, but brawn will keep in a refrigerator for up to 1 week.

Method

Rinse the pig's head in cold water and put into a large pan with the beef, peeled onion (left whole) and bouquet garni. Barely cover with cold water, cover pan closely with a tightly fitting lid, bring to the boil and then simmer for $2\frac{1}{2}$-3 hours or until both head and shin are very tender.

The head is cooked when the bones can be pulled out easily. Cool slightly. Lift meat on to a large dish, strain stock and return to pan, boil gently.

Meanwhile remove bones and pull the meats into pieces with two forks. Pepper well, put meat into the basins. Ladle in enough of the reduced stock to come level with the meat. Leave overnight in a cold larder or refrigerator. Turn out when required, slicing fairly thinly to serve. A sharp dressing (see left) or Cumberland sauce (see page 101), is good with most rich meats.

Jellied game

3 **pigeons**
1 **rabbit**
**'wings' and legs of a hare (about
    1 lb), or equivalent weight of
    venison, or lean pork**
1 **pheasant, or any game bird in
    season**
1 **large onion (peeled)**
1 **carrot**
large bouquet garni
strip of lemon rind
salt and pepper
½ lb cooked ham (sliced)

For forcemeat balls
¾ lb pork sausage meat
1 **tablespoon chopped parsley**
2 **tablespoons breadcrumbs**
1 **egg white (lightly stirred)**
stock (for poaching)

For jelly
stock (from the game)
1 **glass golden sherry, or port, per
    quart of stock (optional)**
1½ oz gelatine

This quantity serves 10-12 people.

Method
Wipe all the game and put into a large pan. Add peeled onion and carrot whole, bouquet garni and lemon rind. Season and just cover with cold water. Cover pan and simmer for 1½-2 hours until game is tender.

Meanwhile prepare force-meat balls : mix meat, parsley, crumbs and season ; bind with egg white. Shape, lay in a wide shallow pan (only one layer). Just cover balls with stock or water, put lid on pan, poach gently for 12-15 minutes. Remove from heat, leave in the liquid to cool, then lift out carefully.

Take game from pan, pull into small slices with two forks, discarding any skin or bones. Strain the stock and return to pan. Add the sherry or port and extra seasoning, if necessary ; reduce by boiling gently until strong and well-flavoured. Dissolve gelatine in 1 quart of this stock. Allow to cool.

Layer game, shredded ham and forcemeat balls in dishes. Gently pour in enough of cool jellied stock just to cover. Leave until next day to set, or keep up to 2-3 days in refrigerator.

Watchpoint Make sure that game simmers but doesn't boil, and when stock reduces that it doesn't boil hard and cloud jelly. Keep well skimmed.

Raised pork pie

1 lb pork (lean and fat mixed)
salt and pepper
1 rounded teaspoon mixed dried
    herbs
$\frac{1}{4}$ pint jellied stock (made from pork
    bones — see method, page 139)

For hot water crust
1 lb plain flour
1 teaspoon salt
7 oz lard
$7\frac{1}{2}$ fl oz milk and water (mixed in
    equal proportions)
milk (for glaze) — optional

1 jar (eg. Kilner jar)

This quantity serves 4 people.

Method

Dice pork for filling, season well and add herbs. Set oven at 350°F or Mark 4.

For hot water crust : warm a mixing bowl and sift in flour and salt, make a well in the centre of the flour.

Heat lard in milk and water. When just boiling, pour into the well in the flour, stir quickly with a wooden spoon until thick, then work with the hand to a dough. Turn on to a board or table, cut off a quarter of the dough, put it back in the warm bowl and cover with a cloth.

Pat out the rest of dough with the fist to a thick round, set a large jar in the centre and work dough up sides. Let dough cool then gently lift out jar. Fill dough case with meat mixture. Roll or pat out remaining dough to form a lid, leave a small hole in it, then put on top of pie, seal edges. Glaze with milk if wished.

Slide pie on to a baking sheet and bake in pre-set oven for 1-1$\frac{1}{2}$ hours. If pie is getting too brown, cover with damp grease-proof paper towards end of cooking time. Leave till cool before placing a funnel in hole in lid and filling up with jellied stock.

Watchpoint You must work quickly and mould pastry while it is still warm, otherwise lard sets and pastry becomes brittle.

To make a raised pork pie case : work dough up sides of jar while it is still warm

Cumberland sauce

Remove rind from a quarter of 1 orange with potato peeler. Cut into long fine shreds and cook in boiling water until tender, then drain and rinse well. Dissolve 4 tablespoons of redcurrant jelly (see page 136) over gentle heat, then stir in juice of $\frac{1}{2}$ a lemon, 1 wineglass of port wine and strained orange juice. When cold, add orange rind and serve.

Pressed tongue

1 ox tongue (4½-6 lb)
cold salted water
1 large carrot
1 large onion (peeled)
6-8 peppercorns
1-2 bayleaves

Tongue press (available in two sizes), or round cake tin, or soufflé dish

This quantity serves 4-6 people.

Method

Put the tongue into a large pan, cover well with cold salted water. Bring slowly to the boil, then add other ingredients. Cover pan and simmer gently for 4-5 hours, or until the tongue is very tender.

Test by trying to pull out the small bone at the base of the tongue — if it comes away easily the tongue is done. It is also advisable to stick the point of a knife into the thickest part (just above the root). It will slip in easily if the meat is cooked.

Cool in the liquid, then lift out the tongue and put in a bowl of cold water. This will make it easier to handle.

Peel off the skin, cut away a little of the root and remove any bones. Curl the tongue round and push into the tongue press, cake tin or soufflé dish. The tongue must fit closely into the tin or dish. Press down well, using a small plate with a weight on top, if no press is available. Leave in a cool place until the next day before turning out. Cover the tongue and store in larder or refrigerator (can be kept for up to 1 week).

Watchpoint It is almost impossible to overcook a tongue so you should always give it the benefit of the doubt. If even slightly undercooked it can be rubbery. Cumberland sauce (see page 101) makes a good accompaniment.

1 *Remove skin from the cooked tongue after it has been cooled*
2 *Press the tongue well down into the tin so that it fits snugly*
3 *Make sure that the press on the tongue is as tight as possible*

Galantine of veal

3-4 lb breast of veal (boned)
2 onions (quartered)
2 carrots (quartered)
large bouquet garni

For farce
6 oz cooked ham (minced)
8 oz pork (minced)
1 small onion (finely chopped)
1 oz butter
1½ teacups fresh white breadcrumbs
1 small egg (beaten)
salt and pepper
6-8 pistachio nuts (blanched and
    shredded, see page 135)

*Large needle and coarse thread ;
    scalded cloth*

This quantity serves 6-8 people.

Method
First prepare the veal farce. Thoroughly mix minced ham and pork together in a bowl. Cook finely chopped onion in butter until soft but not coloured. Add to meat mixture with breadcrumbs, bind with beaten egg. Season well, add pistachio nuts.

Spread stuffing on cut surface of veal, roll up and sew with thread or tie securely. Wrap in greaseproof paper and then in a piece of scalded cloth. Tie at each end and fasten cloth in centre with a safety-pin.

Put into a large pan of boiling water with prepared vegetables and bouquet garni. Cover and simmer for 1½ hours. Take out meat, cool a little and tighten cloth as much as possible. Put meat into a deep dish. Rest a board or enamel plate, with a 2 lb weight on it, on top of the meat to press lightly. Leave overnight. Then remove board, cloth and paper and brush with meat glaze (see page 98).

Boned, stuffed veal is sewn up with thread before wrapping in a piece of scalded cloth (or you can first wrap the meat in greaseproof paper)

The cloth is then securely fastened with a safety-pin before placing the wrapped meat in the pan of boiling water with the vegetables and herbs

Pineapple charlotte

1 pint milk
4 egg yolks
1 teaspoon arrowroot
2 rounded tablespoons caster sugar
1 medium-size can pineapple rings
½ pint double cream
scant ¾ oz gelatine
2 egg whites
1 packet langues de chats biscuits

*7-inch diameter spring-form cake tin
(a catch unclips to open sides)*

This quantity serves 4 people.

Method

Scald milk in a pan. Cream egg yolks in a bowl with arrowroot and sugar, pour on milk and return to pan. Stir over heat to thicken, but do not boil. Strain custard and cool.

Drain pineapple (keep juice); chop up 2 rings (to give 3-4 tablespoons of chopped pineapple) and keep rest for decoration. Lightly whip cream.

Soak gelatine in 4 tablespoons pineapple juice, dissolve over heat, then add to custard with three-quarters of cream. Whisk egg whites until stiff.

As custard begins to thicken, fold in egg whites with chopped pineapple, using a metal spoon. Turn at once into cake tin. When set, turn out and spread sides of charlotte with remaining cream; arrange biscuits on cream, overlapping slightly. Decorate top with rest of pineapple and additional cream.

Hedgehog tipsy cake

1 sponge, or madeira, cake
2 wineglasses sweet white wine
1 glass sweet sherry
1 wineglass fruit syrup
2 oz almonds (blanched and
   shredded — see page 134)
apricot glaze (see page 133)

For syllabub
2 large oranges
1 lemon
2-3 oz caster sugar
½ pint double cream

7½-inch oval fluted jelly mould (for home-made cake)

Ingredients above are solely for this size jelly mould. This quantity serves 4 people.

Method
The cake can be bought or home-made, but must be stale. If home-made, make cake in an oval jelly mould. Trim to resemble shape of a hedgehog's back and hollow out top with a round cutter, reserving the cut-out piece. Then set the cake on a serving dish.

Mix wines and syrup together in a bowl and pour into hollow in cake. As liquids run through, baste the cake well so that it is thoroughly soaked. Put back cut-out piece of cake and baste again. Leave overnight.

Blanch and shred almonds. Spread shredded almonds on a baking sheet and bake to a golden-brown in oven at 350°F or Mark 4. Heat apricot glaze and brush over cake. Stick almonds into cake on top and sides, sloping all one way to resemble quills. Start at the back and continue all the way up to the 'nose'.

To make syllabub; squeeze juice from oranges and lemon separately and measure. There should be one-quarter the quantity of lemon to orange. Dissolve sugar in mixed juices in a pan over low heat, remove from heat, allow to cool. Start to whisk cream and when thickening pour in liquid. Continue to whisk until thick, then spoon round hedgehog cake.

Port wine jelly

1 pint port wine (about ¾ bottle)
½-inch piece stick of cinnamon
2 strips of lemon rind
4 oz lump sugar
2 oz gelatine
¾ pint water

Jelly mould (decorative china may be used, or, traditionally, tin-lined copper)

This quantity serves 4 people.

Method
Pour half the port into a scrupulously clean saucepan. Bring to the boil, simmer for 2-3 minutes, then add flavourings and sugar. Set aside to infuse for 10 minutes.

Soak gelatine in the water, leave 2-3 minutes, then pour into the pan containing the flavoured port. Heat gently to dissolve gelatine, then add rest of port. Strain, pour into jelly mould (previously rinsed out in cold water) and leave to set. Dip mould into warm water to turn out the jelly.

Milk jelly

1½ pints creamy milk
pared rind of 1 lemon
2 oz gelatine
¼ pint water
¼ pint cream

Jelly mould

This quantity serves 4 people.

Method
Heat lemon rind in milk, then leave to infuse for 7-10 minutes. Soak gelatine in water for 2-3 minutes. Add to milk and stir until dissolved. Strain into jelly mould (previously rinsed out in cold water), leave to set. Turn out, pour the cream round before serving.

Danish open sandwiches

These are useful for informal party entertaining or casual family meals. Their charm, when eaten, is that they have plenty of topping on very little bread ; their impact on the eye depends on careful arrangement of the ingredients. Overleaf are recipes for the sandwiches on the large board shown in the photograph below.

Sandwiches on the platter include salami, chicken, liver pâté, egg and caviar, and luncheon meat (clockwise from metal slice). On the table are some ingredients for more Danish sandwiches : wheatmeal, white and Danish rye bread ; prunes ; grilled bacon ; Mycella, Esrom, Danablu and Samsoe cheeses ; fresh vegetables ; Danish butter ; Russian salad ; mayonnaise ; and Danish bacon

Danish open sandwiches

Chicken and bacon

chicken joints
white bread (sliced and buttered)
lettuce leaves
1 streaky bacon roll (grilled) for
each slice of bread
1 orange (thinly sliced)
sprigs of watercress

Method
Fry the chicken joints slowly in butter until golden-brown and tender, allowing 8-10 minutes on each side for legs and a little less for breasts. Allow to cool.

Cover each slice of bread with a lettuce leaf, place a chicken joint on top with a bacon roll alongside. Make a cut in a slice of orange, twist or curl it like a butterfly and lay it carefully on the chicken ; tuck a sprig of watercress between the chicken and bacon.

Liver pâté

1 slice liver pâté for each slice
of bread
rye bread (thinly sliced and well
buttered)
French mustard
1 cocktail sausage for each slice
of bread
tomatoes (sliced)
gherkins

Method
Spread the buttered bread with a little of the mustard and then cover with a slice of liver pâté. Garnish each sandwich with a cocktail sausage (cut in half), two slices of tomato and a gherkin, cut into a fan shape.

Hard-boiled egg and caviar

wholemeal bread (sliced and
buttered)

For each slice of bread use :
1 lettuce leaf
4 slices of hard-boiled egg
4 slices of tomato
1 tablespoon mayonnaise
1 tablespoon Danish caviar
tomato snippets

Method
Cover each slice of bread with a lettuce leaf and arrange the slices of egg with the tomato on the lettuce. Spoon the mayonnaise down the centre and top this with the caviar. Scatter on the tomato snippets.

Luncheon meat

pork luncheon meat (sliced)
rye crispbread (buttered)
horseradish cream (made with 2
tablespoons horseradish sauce,
1 teaspoon sugar, a squeeze of
lemon juice and a 6 fl oz can of
Danish cream)
lettuce heart
1 orange (sliced)
2 cooked prunes (stoned) for each
slice of bread

Method
Fold each slice of luncheon meat in half and arrange on the buttered crispbread, using 3 slices for each sandwich. Put a spoonful of horseradish cream on the top, with a small piece of lettuce heart beside it. Twist the slice of orange and place it on the luncheon meat with a prune on either side.

Ices and summer drinks

Commercial ices may be good, but home-made ones are still better! For a true cream ice you will need a special churn freezer, but there are many delicious sorbets and iced puddings you can make equally well in a refrigerator or home-freezer. And to quench a summer thirst go for home-made fruit drinks, chilled wine cups and flavoured milk punches.

How to make cream and water ices

At one time ices and iced puddings were always made at home with a manual machine, but when 'bought' ice-cream became obtainable everywhere, ice-cream making became rather a lost art. Now, however, when both manual and electric ice-cream makers are available and many people have refrigerators, if not a home-freezer, home-made ices are back in favour. Home-made cream and water ices are completely different both in flavour and texture from the bought varieties ; many people appreciate this and are more than willing to give that little extra time and trouble to making them and to investing in a special machine. Though cream or water ices can be made in the ice cube trays (minus the cube divisions) of the refrigerator, they haven't the quality or velvety texture of one that is made in a machine, where the mixture is churned or beaten continually while freezing. To be really good, ices should be made an hour or more before serving and left in the tray or container. Alternatively, they can be moulded and deep-frozen.

Methods of freezing

In refrigerator or home-freezer. Use the ice trays of a refrigerator or a stainless steel bowl in a home-freezer. In both these cases, the mixture must be well stirred about every hour and, as it thickens, stirred and beaten more frequently until it barely holds its shape. Then smooth over the top and cover with foil. Leave for at least an hour to 'ripen' (see page 114) before serving.

For freezing a water ice in the refrigerator, see lemon water ice (basic recipe) on page 116.

Churn freezer. This type can be manual or electric. The former is more generally used, and it consists of a wooden bucket with a metal container fitted with a dasher (see photographs). The bucket is first packed with a combination of ice and salt, and the ice-cream mixture is poured into the container. A handle is then turned which revolves the dasher, and so not only gradually scrapes away the mixture from round the sides as it freezes, but also churns, or beats, it at the same time.

The electric churn machines, of which there are two types, operate on the same principle. On type is set in the ice-making compartment of the refrigerator (so that there is no necessity for extra ice), with the flex leading to an electric plug outside the refrigerator. The other variety requires a quantity of ice.

The hand churn freezer is moderate in price and, if well cared for, will last for several years. The electric churn freezers are naturally more expensive. The hand churn freezer is made in different sizes from 1 quart upwards (ice-cream being

Equipment for ice-cream making, from top left : refrigerator ice-cube trays, pail holding ice and ice pick, nylon strainer, stainless steel bowl, hand-operated ice-cream churn, electric churn for use in refrigerator, bombe moulds, and ice-cream scoop

How to make cream and water ices

measured by the quart). A 2-quart machine is the most convenient size for the average household.

The mixture to be frozen must not come more than half to three-quarters of the way up the sides of the container. This allows for what is called 'swell', ie. when the cream mixture is churned the quantity increases and rises in the container. A water ice has slightly less swell, and it is not apparent until the egg white has been added (see lemon water ice, page 116).

To obtain a low freezing temperature a mixture of ice and salt is used. The salt should be coarse rock salt (known as freezing salt), obtainable from some fishmongers and from big stores. The ice is best chipped off from a block rather than ice made by an ice-maker. The latter is in pellets (or small cubes), which are uneconomical as churn freezers require constant refilling. Being small, the pellets melt very quickly. As they are usually square, they do not, therefore, fit well around the machine.

Unfortunately, with the wider use of refrigerators and home-freezers, many fishmongers only stock ice made by an ice-maker. Those who are fortunate enough to possess a roomy home-freezer can freeze water in any suitable container, break or chip it into convenient-sized pieces, then store it in polythene bags for future use.

To chip ice, use an ice pick, consisting of a single spike fitted into a wooden handle. To break the ice, put the block on several layers of newspaper on the floor, or if more convenient in the sink. Give short sharp jabs at the piece or block of ice with the pick ; avoid going right through down to the paper.

Watchpoint The pieces of ice should not be so large that the salt trickles through the gaps between them, as would certainly happen if ice cubes from the refrigerator were used. This can be prevented if the pieces are well jabbed down with the pick when filling them into the bucket.

Care of churn freezer

After use the container, lid and dasher must be washed well, then scalded with boiling water. Dry container thoroughly before putting it away with its lid off. Keep the ratchet well oiled to ensure smooth running and to avoid squeaking. Rinse the bucket well in cold water, then dry. If the machine has not been used for some time it is wise, when you start using it again, to immerse the bucket in cold water for a few hours to enable the wood to swell and so keep it comparatively water-tight.

Packing the churn

Make sure that the container and dasher are well rinsed with boiling water so that both are scrupulously clean and free from smell.

Assemble the machine by inserting the dasher in the container, putting on the lid and setting it in the centre of the bucket. Fix the centre bar and ratchet in and over the container to hold it in position.

Now fill the sides of the bucket with ice and freezing

salt, approximately 1 part salt to 3 parts ice. A large cup makes a convenient measure. Start with a bottom layer of ice, then salt and continue until the mixture is about 2 inches below the lid of the container, ending with the ice. Pack the ice and salt down well with the ice pick. Give the handle a turn to make sure it runs freely, and brush away any salt which may have fallen on the lid or edge of the bucket.

Now carefully remove the centre bar and lid and pour in the mixture to be frozen. Fill no more than half to a bare three-quarters full.

Place a piece of greaseproof paper over the top of the con-tainer (an added precaution against any salt getting into the mixture) and replace the lid and centre bar.

Leave for 2-3 minutes before starting to turn the handle. Set the machine on a stool or chair, first covering the seat ▶

1 Inserting the dasher in the hand-operated churn; the lid, ratchet and handle are at side
2 Packing in layers of ice and freezing salt after replacing the clean lid and handle
3 Pouring a cream ice mixture, ready for churning, into the container surrounded by ice
4 Placing greaseproof paper over the top of the container before replacing the lid and handle

How to make cream and water ices
continued

well with newspaper. This comparatively low position makes for easier working. Have additional ice and salt at hand for refilling.

How to churn
Start by turning the handle smoothly and evenly for about 3 minutes. Then leave for a further 3-4 minutes. Test the handle again, and if it shows any resistance continue to churn until the handle is really stiff to turn round. If the mixture is made with the right proportion of sugar, the time for churning should not exceed 5-6 minutes.

In the early stages, a cream mixture can be left in the container longer than 3 minutes, and water ices up to 5 minutes. This allows the mixture to get really cold and therefore shortens the time of churning. During this period, test the handle every minute or so and, as soon as resistance is felt, start at once to churn regularly. Keep the bucket topped up with ice and salt, if necessary, but do this during the initial period, before the main churning.

When ice is really stiff, stop churning and pour off any water from the hole in the side of the bucket. Wipe lid free of any water or salt, then remove the centre bar and lid carefully and lift up dasher with one hand, holding the container down with the other. Scrape the dasher free from mixture with a plastic scraper or table knife. Push mixture down from around the sides into the bottom of the container.

Cover the top with a piece of foil, or double sheet of grease-proof paper, and replace the lid. Bung the hole in the lid with a screw of paper and fill up the bucket with more ice and salt. Cover the top with a thick cloth ; use a floor or oven cloth or a piece of sacking. Set the churn in a cool place and leave for 1 hour or longer. If left for longer than 1 hour, however, the melted ice will have to be drained off and the bucket replenished with ice.

How to ripen : this leaving of the ice mixture, which applies particularly to cream ices, is to allow it to ripen or mellow, which greatly improves both the flavour and texture.

Watchpoint It is important to avoid the handle getting stuck. This occurs if the mixture has been left too long in the packed machine during the first stage or if the later churning has been interrupted. Too much pressure put on the handle results in damaging the cogs in the ratchet and possibly breaking the wooden flanges of the dasher. It is equally important to avoid any grain of salt or salty water getting into the mixture, hence the necessity to wipe the lid clean before removing it.

Serving the finished ice

Whether making cream or water ices, it is wise to invest in an ice scoop. This makes the job easier and also gives an indication as to how much ice-cream to make. These scoops are numbered on the handle, 18-20 etc., thus indicating the number of scoops obtainable from 1 quart of ice-cream.

To serve, have a jug of cold

water ready alongside the container, dip the scoop in the water and then into the ice mixture. When full, level off the scoop with a knife or against the side of the container. Hold it over the dish or coupe glass and press the spring on the handle which releases the ice mixture. Then dip the scoop into the water and repeat the process.

Sugar content

The amount of sugar in the mixture to be frozen is important — whether for a cream or water ice. Too sweet a mixture will not freeze ; one not sweet enough gives a hard and tasteless ice. Though to a certain extent this can be corrected once the mixture is made, it is wise to start working to a definite proportion (as given in the basic recipes).

The proportion of sugar is even more important in a water ice than a cream one to give the right soft, yet firm, consistency. It helps to test by tasting, but keep on the sweet side, especially if there is a fruit base, eg. raspberry, blackcurrant or pineapple. The flavour is weakened by freezing, so always taste the mixture before pouring it into the container.

Water ices

A water ice is essentially a fruit-flavoured, light syrup, either lemon or orange, or a fruit purée with syrup added. This type is best churned in a freezer, but it can be made in a refrigerator if a small quantity of gelatine is added.

Water ice is frozen to a slush before a very small quantity of egg white, whipped to a firm snow, is added and the freezing is continued until the ice is firm. The addition of egg white binds the ice together and makes for a smooth, yet firm, consistency.

The term 'sorbet' originally referred to a Turkish iced drink. Today, bought water ices are often called sorbets, probably because the name is more attractive commercially.

A true sorbet has a lemon or orange water ice base flavoured with liqueur, with Italian meringue added. A sorbet used to be served between the entrée and roast during a long menu, and was designed to clean the palate and refresh the stomach in preparation for the courses which were to follow.

Adding a little whipped egg white to the churn when making water ice

Lemon water ice

1¼ pints water
pared rind and juice of 3 large
    and juicy lemons
7 oz lump sugar
½ egg white (whisked)
scant ½ oz gelatine

This recipe gives the basic
method for making water ices.

Method

Put the water, lemon rind and
sugar into a scrupulously clean
pan, bring slowly to the boil,
simmer for 5 minutes, then
strain into a jug ; add strained
lemon juice, mix well and taste
for sweetness. Chill well.

Pour chilled mixture into the
packed freezer, leave for 5 minutes, then churn to a slush. Whip
egg white to a firm snow and
add $\frac{3}{4}$-1 tablespoon toice, then
churn it until firm. Remove
dasher and pack down.

Note : if freezing the ice in a
refrigerator, dissolve the gelatine
in a small quantity of the sugar
syrup after straining it. Add to
the jug with the lemon juice. Chill
before pouring into the ice
trays. Turn the refrigerator
down to the maximum freezing
temperature, freeze to a slush,
then beat in the required amount
of white. Return to the ice
compartment, freeze until just
firm, then beat again, cover
with foil and return to the ice
compartment. Turn refrigerator
back to normal and leave the
ice until required.

Watchpoint The quantity of
egg white varies according to
consistency desired for individual recipes. Half a white is
the smallest quantity it is possible to whisk, but it may not be
necessary to use it all.

Pineapple water ice

1 large pineapple
soft fruits (see method)

For ice
6 oz lump sugar
1 pint water
pared rind and juice of 1 large
    lemon
½ egg white (whisked)

To garnish
vine, or strawberry, leaves

Method

Dissolve the sugar in the water
with the pared rind of the lemon
and boil for 4-5 minutes ; then
add the lemon juice, strain, and
leave liquid to cool.

Split the pineapple in two,
lengthways, and slice out the
pulp with a grapefruit knife,
removing the large centre core.
With a fork break the flesh of
the pineapple into shreds and
measure this. There should be
$\frac{3}{4}$-1 pint. Add this pulp to the
cold syrup and freeze as for
lemon water ice (left),
adding 1 tablespoon whisked
egg white when it forms a slush.

Chill the pineapple halves
and, when ready to serve, put
the fresh soft fruits, eg. raspberries, strawberries or currants,
in the bottom of the pineapple
halves and set the ice on top.
Arrange the pineapple halves
on a silver dish lined with green
leaves, such as vine leaves or
strawberry leaves.

A selection of home-made ices : pineapple water ice, served in pineapple halves on a bed of green leaves ; plum pudding ice decorated with a ruff of flavoured, whipped cream ; vanilla cream ice and grapefruit mint ice

Orange water ice

4 large oranges
pared rind and juice of 2 lemons
8 oz lump sugar
1½ pints water
½ egg white (whisked)

Method
Put the rind of the lemon into a pan with 6 oz sugar and the water and dissolve over heat. Draw pan aside, then rub the remaining lumps of sugar on to the rind of the oranges to remove the zest. Do this thoroughly. Return the pan to the heat and boil mixture for a further 5 minutes, then draw pan aside, add the lumps of sugar, allow them to dissolve and return pan to heat for about 30 seconds. Remove pan from heat, take out lemon rind and add the strained juice of the lemons and oranges to the mixture and chill.

Pour mixture into a churn freezer and churn as directed in the general instructions. Add 1 dessertspoon to 1 tablespoon of the egg white, whisked to a firm snow, when the ice is frozen to a slush. Continue to churn until firm then pack down. The ice is now ready to serve.

Blackcurrant leaf water ice

4 large handfuls of blackcurrant
  leaves
pared rind and juice of 3 large
  lemons
7 oz lump sugar
1½ pints water
2-3 drops of edible green colouring
½ egg white (whisked)

This ice is sometimes called 'muscat ice' as the infusion of blackcurrant leaves gives the ice a strong flavour of muscat grapes.

Method
Put the rind into a scrupulously clean pan with the lump sugar and the water. Dissolve sugar completely, then boil rapidly for 5 minutes and add the washed blackcurrant leaves. Cover the pan and draw off the heat. Allow liquid to infuse until well flavoured, then strain, squeezing the leaves well to extract all the syrup. Add the strained lemon juice and the colouring.

Freeze mixture and, when it is a slush, add 1 dessertspoon of egg white, whisked to a firm snow. Stir in, or churn, remaining egg white, then continue to freeze until firm. Serve either plain or with sugared fruit, or with Charentais melon (see below.

For an unusual first course serve either Charentais melons cut in half, with the seeds removed, and a scoop of muscat, or blackcurrant leaf, water ice placed in the centre ; or grapefruit halves topped with mint water ice.

Grapefruit with mint ice

3 **grapefruit**
¾ **pint water**
pared rind and juice of 2 large
   lemons
4 **oz lump sugar**
2 **large handfuls of mint leaves**
   (picked from the stalk)
2-3 **drops of edible green colouring**
   (optional)
½ **egg white (whisked)**

To garnish
caster sugar
freshly chopped mint, or 1-2
   leaves of crystallised mint

Method

First prepare the ice. Put the water into a pan with the pared rind of the lemons and the sugar. Bring to the boil and cook for 4-5 minutes. Draw pan aside, add the well-washed mint leaves and the juice of the lemons.

Watchpoint Leave pan on the side of the stove for liquid to infuse ; do not boil as this would spoil the flavour.

After 10-12 minutes, strain liquid into a jug, taste for sweetness and add colour, if wished. Chill and then freeze ice, either in a churn or in the ice-making compartment of the refrigerator. When the ice is just frozen to a slush, add 1 teaspoon of whisked egg white.

Prepare the grapefruit in the usual way and hollow out the centres a little to hold the ice. Dust with caster sugar and chill.

To serve, put a scoop of the ice on the centre of each grapefruit and sprinkle with a little freshly-chopped mint or 1-2 crystallised mint leaves.

Crystallised mint leaves

Pick some fresh mint leaves, brush them very lightly with lightly broken egg white. Dust with caster sugar and place on greaseproof paper or a cake rack to dry for 1-2 hours. These will not keep for more than a day.

119

Raspberry water ice

2 lb raspberries
2-3 tablespoons icing sugar
½ egg white (whisked)

For ½ pint sugar syrup
7 fl oz water
6 oz granulated sugar

Method

Make the sugar syrup by dissolving sugar in the water over gentle heat, then boiling for 3-4 minutes. Leave this syrup to get cold.

Purée the raspberries by either rubbing them through a nylon sieve or putting them in a blender. If using a blender, strain the purée to get rid of any pieces of seed. Add about 2-3 tablespoons icing sugar to purée to sweeten it lightly.

Gradually add the cold sugar syrup to the purée, stirring well. Taste for sweetness, then chill. Turn ice into a churn freezer and churn until it forms a slush. Then whisk the egg white and add 1 tablespoon of this to the mixture. Continue to churn the ice, and when it is really firm remove dasher and pack down.

Note : 1 lb of juicy raspberries should yield about 7-8 fl oz, thus 2 lb should make just under 1 pint. If a little short on quantity, extra syrup can be added ; do this while making the raspberries into a purée, rinsing off the purée from the sieve or the sides of the blender with the sugar syrup. Taste for strength of flavour and sweetness.

Cream ices

Cream ices are made on a base of either egg mousse or custard, with a proportion of egg white added. When the mousse or custard is cold, cream is folded into the mixture.

For cream ices made on an egg mousse base, single cream can be used. If using double cream, partially whip it to give the ice a smoother and richer consistency, especially when freezing ice in refrigerator.

As with water ices, freezing diminishes the flavour and colour of cream ices, so this must always be taken into consideration when tasting the unfrozen mixture.

Vanilla cream ice 1

2 eggs
2 egg yolks
3 oz caster sugar
1 pint milk
1 vanilla pod, or 2-3 drops of
   vanilla essence
¼ pint single cream, or double cream
   (lightly whipped)

This is the basic method for making cream ices on a custard base.

The caster sugar may be flavoured with a vanilla pod. This is done by leaving a dry pod in a small jar of caster sugar for a few days. The vanilla in the recipe may then be omitted.

Method
Break the whole eggs into a bowl, add the separated egg yolks, then the sugar and whisk to mix well, but not so that the mixture becomes slushy.

Scald the milk (if using a vanilla pod, split it and add to the milk). When it is at boiling point, pour on the egg mixture, stirring vigorously. Strain custard and allow to cool. If using vanilla essence, add it at this point.

When custard is quite cold, add the cream, then freeze it in the refrigerator ice tray, or in a churn freezer.

Vanilla cream ice 2

1 vanilla pod, or vanilla essence
1¼ pints single, or double, cream
3 oz granulated sugar
4 fl oz water
4 egg yolks (well beaten)

This ice is made on an egg mousse base and is more suitable for making in a refrigerator than vanilla cream ice 1.

Method
Split the vanilla pod and scoop out a few seeds. Put the cream into a pan with the vanilla pod. Leave it to infuse, covered, for about 7-10 minutes on a low heat until the cream is well scalded, ie. just below simmering point. Strain cream, cover with greaseproof paper to prevent a skin from forming and leave to cool.

Put the sugar and the water into a small pan, stir over gentle heat until the sugar is dissolved, then boil steadily without shaking or stirring until a drop of cooled syrup will form a thread between your finger and thumb.

Have the well-beaten egg yolks ready, then draw pan of syrup aside and, when the bubbles have subsided, pour it on to the yolks and whisk well with a rotary whisk until the mixture is thick and mousse-like. Add the cream and vanilla essence, if used, and mix well. Chill mixture thoroughly before freezing it.

Note : alternatively use half double and half single cream, but do not scald. Partly whip the double cream and add it to the mousse with the single cream.

Chocolate cream ice

7 oz plain block chocolate
2 oz granulated sugar
4 fl oz water
3 egg yolks (well beaten)
vanilla essence, rum or brandy
    (to flavour) — optional
1¼ pints single cream

A chocolate cream ice is usually flavoured with vanilla, unless rum or brandy is added.

Method
Put sugar and water into a pan, dissolve sugar over gentle heat, then boil steadily until the cooled syrup will form a thread between your finger and thumb. Have the well-beaten yolks ready, carefully pour syrup on to them, whisk to a thick mousse-like mixture, add flavouring ; then set aside.

Break up the chocolate, put into a pan with the cream and dissolve slowly over gentle heat. Bring it to scalding point, then draw pan aside and allow to cool, then add to mousse. Chill mixture before freezing.
Note : if wished, half single and half double cream may be used. In this case dissolve the chocolate as before in the single cream and, when added to the egg mousse, lightly whip the double cream and add this to the mixture, then freeze.

> **Chocolate cream ices** can also be made using the vanilla cream ice 1 recipe (see page 121). Take the same quantity of chocolate as above, dissolve it in the milk, then add mixture to egg yolks.

Brown bread cream ice

vanilla cream ice 2 (see page 121)
about ¾ of stale brown loaf
caster sugar
Melba sauce (see page 54)

Method
Remove crusts from bread and make bread into crumbs. Sprinkle with caster sugar and toast crumbs until a good brown in a hot oven at 375°F or Mark 5. This should make 6 tablespoons. Leave to get cold.

Churn the vanilla cream ice until almost set, then quickly add the crumbs and continue to churn for 1-2 minutes. Pack down and leave to ripen.

Serve ice on a chilled dish with the sauce.

Fruit cream ice

1 pint fruit purée (lightly
   sweetened)
4 oz granulated sugar
scant $\frac{1}{4}$ pint water
3 egg yolks (well beaten)
$\frac{3}{4}$ pint single cream

The fruit purée may be made
with raspberries, apricots or
blackcurrants, etc., and if using
a strong-flavoured fruit, such
as blackcurrants or damsons,
add more sugar than you would
to, say, a strawberry purée.

Method

For the fruit purée : damsons
and other firm fruit such as
gooseberries or apricots should
be first cooked and then made
into a purée. Soft fruit, such as
raspberries and strawberries,
can be made into a purée when
raw ; if done in a blender, strain
this purée before use.

Prepare an egg mousse with
the sugar, water and yolks as
for vanilla cream ice 2 (see page
121). When cool, add the cream
and purée. Taste to make sure
it is sufficiently sweet. Freeze as
for other cream ices.

Plum pudding ice

2 oz currants
4 oz stoned raisins
$\frac{1}{2}$ oz blanched almonds
$\frac{1}{2}$ oz candied orange peel
1 oz glacé cherries
$\frac{1}{2}$ wineglass brandy, or rum

For cream ice mixture
6 oz plain block chocolate, or 2 oz
   cocoa and 2$\frac{1}{2}$ fl oz cold water
1 pint single, or $\frac{1}{2}$ pint single and
   $\frac{1}{2}$ pint double, cream
2 oz granulated sugar
2$\frac{1}{2}$ fl oz water
3 egg yolks

Method

First prepare the fruit. Wash the
currants and raisins well, finely
shred the almonds and candied
orange peel and rinse the
cherries to get rid of some of the
heavy syrup. Pour over the
brandy (or rum) and leave fruit
to macerate for 1-2 hours.

To prepare the cream ice
mixture : dissolve chocolate in
the single cream over gentle
heat. If using cocoa, mix with
the cold water and cook to a
thick cream, then add this to the
single cream and scald.

Make an egg mousse with
the sugar, water and yolks (see
vanilla cream ice 2, page 121)
and add to the cream ; if using
double cream, whip it lightly.

When the mixture is chilled,
turn it into a churn freezer and
churn until very thick. Then add
the fruit and continue to churn
until really firm. Remove the
dasher and pack down.

Serve cream ice on a chilled
serving dish scooped out in the
form of a plum pudding.
Decorate, if wished, with a ruff
of whipped cream, flavoured
with brandy (or rum).

Glace en surprise

2-egg whisked sponge (baked in an 8-inch diameter sandwich tin) — see method, Gâteau Margot, page 97
strawberry cream ice (see fruit cream ice, page 123)

For meringue
2 egg whites
4 oz caster sugar
2-3 drops of vanilla essence
caster sugar (for dusting)

Forcing bag with 8- or 10-cut rose pipe

This recipe is also known as baked Alaska or Norwegian omelet. Any flavoured cream ice may be used, but chocolate, strawberry or raspberry are best.

Method
Have the sponge cake and the cream ice ready made. Choose a plated or silver dish and chill it well. Half fill a large roasting tin with ice and freezing salt and set the dish in this. Set oven at 350°F or Mark 4.

To prepare meringue : whisk the egg whites stiffly, add 2-3 rounded teaspoons of the caster sugar and vanilla essence and whisk again until stiff. Fold in the remaining sugar. Fill into the forcing bag.

Place the sponge cake on the dish, scoop out the cream ice and arrange on top of the sponge. Pipe the meringue over the ice to cover it completely. Dust the meringue well with caster sugar ; leave for 1 minute, then put the cake into pre-set oven. Cook for about 4 minutes or until the meringue is lightly browned. Serve at once.

Iced puddings

Bombes are so called because of their bomb-shape moulds, which are made of tin-lined copper with a screw at the base and a tight-fitting lid. These were so designed for easy burying in a mixture of ice and salt, but nowadays a refrigerator with a large ice-making compartment, or preferably a home-freezer, is used. This means that no lid is necessary provided the top is well covered with foil. Unless the special bombe shape is wanted, the ices in these recipes can be frozen in a cake tin or spring-form tin.

For this type of pudding the ice mixture must first be frozen until really firm, then filled to the brim in the previously chilled mould. If using a bombe mould, grease the edge with lard, cover with greaseproof paper and the lid ; if using a cake tin just cover with foil.

For freezing a bombe in the ice-making compartment of the refrigerator, turn the temperature down to maximum cold ; do this 30 minutes before putting in the mould. Leave the mould in the refrigerator for 4 hours or longer. If freezing it in a home-freezer, 2-3 hours should be long enough.

If the ice-making compartment in your refrigerator will not take a mould, and you have no home-freezer, use a large pail with ice and salt in the same proportion as for the churn freezer. But the mould used must be a bombe, or at least one with a tight-fitting lid. Smear around the edge of the mould with lard, and, if using a bombe, make sure that the screw is tight before burying the mould in ice and salt. Cover the pail with a thick cloth, or piece of blanket, and leave in a cool place for 3-4 hours. Tip off any water when necessary and refill with ice.

To turn out the bombe. If frozen in ice and salt, draw the mould through a large bowl of cold water. Dry and remove lid, replace it, but not tightly, and draw again through a bowl of fresh cold water. Two 'swishings' through the water should be enough. This not only loosens the ice in the mould or tin, but also washes away the salt. Dry again and remove the lid and paper.

To turn out bombe, hold over a dish and release knob at the base

Have the serving dish ready ; it is best to use a well-chilled silver or stainless steel one. Turn the bombe over and un-screw the knob at the base which should release the suction and so cause the ice to drop on to the dish. If bombe does not slide out, wrap a hot cloth around mould or keep your hands on it for about 30 seconds. Draw the mould off gently. Finish the ice with a ruff of cream piped round the base, or pour round a cold sauce : Melba, apricot, choco-late, or as you wish.

To turn out ices set in cake tins and spring-form tins : turn out in the same way as for bombes, but draw them 2-3 times through a bowl of cold water. Dry as before, remove foil, then turn out and decorate.

If you feel ambitious, you may use two differently flavoured ices : one to clothe, or line, the inside of the mould by about 1 inch, the other to fill the centre. Alternatively the centre can be filled with lightly-whipped, sweetened cream. For example, coffee cream ice out-side, and whipped cream, mixed with sliced ginger, inside.

125

Bombe maison

1 jar of preserved ginger
½ pint double cream

For meringue
3 egg whites
6 oz caster sugar

For white coffee cream ice
½ pint single cream
2 oz coffee beans
1 whole egg
1 egg yolk
2 oz caster sugar
½ pint double cream

6-7 inch diameter cake tin with a loose bottom ; non-stick (silicone) kitchen paper

This recipe is sometimes called meringue glacé maison when made in a cake tin ; it can be made in a bombe mould but you will find that the meringue rounds fit a cake tin better.

Method
Line three baking sheets with non-stick (silicone) kitchen paper on which you have drawn three 5½-inch diameter circles. Set oven at 250°F or Mark ½ .

To prepare the meringue : whisk egg whites until stiff and add 3 teaspoons of the measured sugar and continue beating for 1 minute. Fold in the remaining sugar with a tablespoon and then spread or pipe the mixture on to the three circles on the prepared baking sheets. Bake in pre-set oven for about 1 hour or until meringues are dry, crisp and pale biscuit-coloured.

To prepare coffee cream ice : scald the single cream with the coffee beans and infuse until a delicate coffee flavour is obtained. Cream the egg and the extra yolk thoroughly with the sugar until light in colour, strain on the scalded cream and whisk well ; strain again and leave to cool. Whip the double cream very slightly and add to the coffee-flavoured custard.

Meanwhile have churn ready packed with ice and salt. Pour in the custard mixture and churn until thick. Scrape down the container, remove the dasher and leave the mixture to ripen.

Slice the preserved ginger ; whip the cream until thick and fold in the ginger. When the meringue is quite cold line the cake tin with a 1-inch layer of the coffee cream ice, put a round of meringue on the top and cover with a layer of cream and ginger. Continue in this way until the tin is full, filling any space at the sides with cream ice. Cover with foil and keep in the ice-making compartment of a refrigerator, or home-freezer (or a pail of ice, if using a bombe mould) until needed. Remove to refrigerator temperature for 1-2 hours before serving.

Champagne cup

1 bottle of Champagne
1½ fl oz orange curaçao
4 fl oz brandy
little icing sugar
about ¾ pint soda water
good dash of Angostura bitters
small quantity of fruit in season
(sliced)
2-3 sprigs of borage, or mint
(bruised)
few ice cubes

Method
Chill the Champagne well before opening. Mix it with the curaçao and brandy and sweeten with a little icing sugar before adding soda and remaining ingredients.

Claret cup

2 bottles of claret
2½ fl oz brandy
1½ fl oz orange curaçao
1 orange (sliced)
1 rounded tablespoon caster sugar
2-3 sprigs of borage, or lemon
verbena
2-3 strips of cucumber
about 1 teaspoon Angostura bitters
about 1 pint soda water

Method
Mix all ingredients together in a large jug, leaving the soda to the last (this is usually added just before serving). Chill lightly rather than add ice cubes.

Hock cup

2 bottles of hock
1½ fl oz orange curaçao
4 fl oz brandy
good dash of Angostura bitters
about ½ pint soda water
small quantity of fruit in season
(sliced) — eg. pineapple, strawberries, orange, etc.
2-3 sprigs of borage, or mint
(bruised)
few ice cubes

Method
Mix all ingredients (except the ice) about one hour before serving. Add ice just before serving.

Cider cup

2 **pints cider**
¼ **bottle orange squash**
¼ **bottle lemon squash**
½ **pint fruit juice**
½ **glass sherry**
dash of Angostura bitters
few strips of cucumber rind
ice
crushed mint

Method
Place all the ingredients in a large jug. Mix thoroughly and stand in a cool place. Allow to stand for 1-2 hours before serving.

Iced coffee shake

This is a different way of making iced coffee, and one that children usually prefer.

Take very cold milk, add coffee essence to taste and a little sugar, if liked. Whisk, adding a little lightly whipped double cream. Keep it in refrigerator until wanted. A spoonful or two of coffee ice-cream may be added instead of the cream.

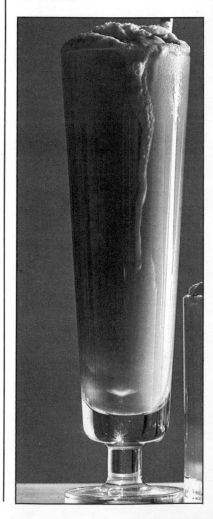

Cold milk punch

1 pint milk
2-3 strips of pared orange, or
  lemon, rind
5-7 tablespoons brandy, or whisky
1 dessertspoon caster sugar
cracked ice

Make this punch in a cocktail shaker or glass jar with a tight-fitting cover. These ingredients make a milk punch for two.

Method
Steep the rind in the spirit for 1-2 hours, pour into the shaker with the milk and sugar. Add a little cracked ice and shake well. Strain off into glasses.

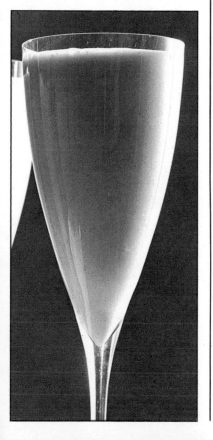

Spiced fruit punch

1 bottle of port, or sherry
1 can (19 fl oz) orange juice
1 can (19 fl oz) pineapple juice
about 1 pint white wine
1 tablespoon granulated sugar
2 strips of lemon peel
1-inch piece of stick cinnamon
2 oranges (sliced)

Method
Put all the ingredients except the sliced orange into a large pan. Simmer for 3-4 minutes. Remove lemon peel and cinnamon stick, pour into punch bowl, add orange slices. Serve with a ladle into warm glasses.

Home-made lemon or orange

3 **lemons (unpeeled and diced)**
3 **tablespoons granulated sugar**
1 **quart boiling water**
sprig of mint (optional)
ice
1-2 **extra slices of lemon**

Method

Wipe lemons and cut into dice — try not to lose any of the juice. Put into a jug (not a glass one) with the sugar. Pour on the boiling water, leave for 15-30 minutes until strong but without the taste becoming bitter ; then strain. Put the mint into the serving jug with the ice and slices of fresh lemon 1 hour before the lemonade is wanted.

To make orange drink : simply squeeze juice from fresh oranges and add sugar to taste.

Orange and tomato cocktail

$\frac{3}{4}$ **pint fresh orange juice (strained)**
2 **pints tomato juice (canned)**
2 **cans vegetable juice (V8)**
3-4 **sprigs of mint**
thinly-pared rind of 1 orange
pinch of salt
pepper (ground from mill)

Method

Mix orange, tomato and vegetable juices together in a large jug. Bruise mint in a bowl, add to the juices with the orange rind and season. Chill well for at least 1 hour, then strain and serve.

Appendix

Notes and basic recipes

Aspic jelly

This is a jelly made of good fish, chicken, or meat stock very slightly sharpened with wine and a few drops of wine vinegar. Care must be taken that the stock is well flavoured and seasoned and that it is not too sharp, only pleasantly acidulated.

Aspic, when properly made, is excellent with fish or meat dishes, but unfortunately it is frequently disliked because it is unpleasantly sharp or tasteless. Aspic acts as a kind of preservative ; food set in or brushed with aspic keeps its attractive appearance and finish for some hours.

With certain delicately flavoured foods, such as fish, eggs or prawns, home-made aspic adds to and enhances the flavour. If you need aspic for brushing over sliced meat, use the commercially prepared variety, which is excellent for this — especially if a small quantity of the water is replaced by sherry. Make up according to directions on the packet or can.

Aspic, and most jellies containing wine, will keep for several days in the refrigerator. To do this, pour the liquid aspic into a jug, leave to set, then pour about ½ inch cold water over the top, and refrigerate. Remember to pour water off before melting the aspic for use.

Basic aspic recipe

2½ fl oz sherry
2½ fl oz white wine
2 oz gelatine
1¾ pints cold stock (see page 139)
1 teaspoon wine vinegar
2 egg whites

Method

Add wines to gelatine and set aside. Pour cold stock into scalded pan, add vinegar. Whisk egg whites to a froth, add them to the pan, set over moderate heat and whisk backwards until the stock is hot. Then add gelatine, which by now will have absorbed the wine, and continue whisking steadily until boiling point is reached.

Stop whisking and allow liquid to rise to the top of the pan ; turn off heat or draw pan aside and leave to settle for about 5 minutes, then bring it again to the boil, draw pan aside once more and leave liquid to settle. At this point the liquid should look clear ; if not, repeat the boiling-up process.

Filter the jelly through a scalded cloth. The aspic should be allowed to cool before use.

Breadcrumbs

To make crumbs : take a large loaf (the best type to use is a sandwich loaf) at least two days old. Cut off the crust and keep to one side. Break up bread into crumbs either by rubbing through a wire sieve or a Mouli sieve, or by working in an electric blender.

Spread crumbs on to a sheet of paper laid on a baking tin and cover with another sheet of paper to keep off any dust. Leave to dry in a warm temperature — the plate rack, or warming drawer, or the top of the oven, or even the airing cupboard, is ideal. The crumbs may take a day or two to dry thoroughly, and they must be crisp before storing in a jar. To make them uniformly find, sift them through a wire bowl strainer.

To make browned crumbs : bake the crusts in a slow oven until golden-brown, then crush or grind through a mincer. Sift and store as for white crumbs. These browned ones are known as raspings and are used for any dish that is coated with a sauce and browned in the oven.

Chantilly cream

Turn ½ pint of double cream into a cold basin and, using a fork or open wire whisk, whisk gently until it thickens. Add 3-4 teaspoons caster sugar to taste and 2-3 drops of vanilla essence and continue whisking until the cream will hold its shape.

For a delicate flavour, instead of the essence, sweeten with vanilla sugar and a few of the seeds scraped from a vanilla pod.

Court bouillon
(2 pint quantity)

2 pints water
1 carrot (sliced)
1 onion (stuck with a clove)
bouquet garni
6 peppercorns
2 tablespoons vinegar
salt

Method
Place all ingredients in a pan, salt lightly and bring to boil. Cover the pan with a lid and simmer for 15-20 minutes. Strain before using.

Fruit glazes

Apricot glaze

For use with all yellow fruit. Make a pound or so at a time as it keeps well and can be used as wanted. Store in a covered jar.

Turn the apricot jam into a saucepan, add the juice of ½ lemon and 4 tablespoons water per lb. Bring slowly to the boil and simmer for 5 minutes. Strain and return to the pan. Boil for a further 5 minutes and turn into a jam jar for keeping. If for immediate use, continue boiling until thick, then brush amply over the fruit. If using a smooth jam (with no lumps of fruit), water is not needed.

Redcurrant glaze

For use with all red fruit. Home-made redcurrant jelly (see page 136) is best as it gives the right sharpness of flavour to the fresh fruit. Beat the jelly with a fork or small whisk until it liquefies, then rub through a strainer into a small saucepan. Heat gently without stirring until quite clear (boiling will spoil both colour and flavour). When brushing this glaze over the fruit use a very soft brush. Always work from the centre outwards, drawing the brush, well laden with the glaze, towards the edge.

Lemon jelly
1¾ oz gelatine
1½ pints water
pared rind of 3 lemons
7½ fl oz lemon juice
2 sticks cinnamon
7 oz lump sugar
whites and shells (wiped and
   lightly crushed) of 2 eggs
2½ fl oz sherry, or water

This basic recipe makes 2 pints of lemon jelly.

Method
Soak gelatine in ¼ pint of the water. Scald a large enamel pan, or an aluminium one with a ground base (use 6 pints capacity pan to allow for boiling). Pour in remaining 1¼ pints of water, and the lemon rind and juice, cinnamon and sugar; warm over gentle heat until sugar is dissolved.

Whip egg whites to a froth, add to the pan with the shells, gelatine and sherry, or water.

Whisk until liquid reaches boiling point, with a backwards (the reverse of the usual whisking movement) and downwards movement. Stop whisking at once and allow liquid to rise well in the pan. At once turn off heat or draw pan aside and leave liquid to settle for about 5 minutes. Bring liquid to the boil two more times, without whisking and drawing pan aside between each boiling to allow it to settle.

By this time a 'filter', or thick white crust, will have formed on top of the liquid. It will be cracked, so that the liquid below is visible. If the liquid is clear, carry on to the next stage ; if it is muddy-looking, bring it to the boil once more.

Have ready a scalded jelly bag with a bowl underneath and turn the contents of the pan into it. Once the jelly begins to run through, take up the bowl (placing another underneath) and pour jelly back into the bag. After a few times the jelly running through should be crystal clear. Then allow it to run through completely before moving bag or bowl. A screw-top jar or jug of hot water placed in the bag helps to keep the jelly liquid.

Watchpoint Lump sugar is best for jelly-making ; it will give a more brilliant jelly as it is less adulterated than the powdered sugar.

Lobster,

To kill a lobster : choose a sharp chopping knife. Lay the lobster out flat on a wooden board, hard shell uppermost. Have the head toward your right hand and cover the tail with a cloth. Hold lobster firmly behind the head with your left hand and with the point of the knife pierce right through the little cross mark which lies on the centre of the head. The lobster is killed at once.

To split a lobster : cut through the top part of the head, turn lobster round and continue to cut through the rear part of the head and down through the tail. Open out the two halves on the board and take out

the dark thread (the intestine) which runs down the tail, and a small sac usually containing weed which lies in the top part of the head. These are the only parts to be thrown away. The greenish part also in the head is the liver which should be retained as it is considered a delicacy.

Nuts

To brown hazelnuts (already shelled) : do not blanch first but bake for 7-8 minutes in a moderate oven at 350°F or Mark 4, then rub briskly in a rough cloth to remove skin. To grind, either chop very finely or grind in a Mouli grater.

Almonds : buy them with their skins on. This way they retain their oil better. Blanching to remove the skins gives extra juiciness.

To blanch almonds : pour boiling water over the shelled nuts, cover the pan and leave until cool. Then the skins can be easily removed (test one with finger and thumb). Drain, rinse in cold water and press skins off with fingers. Rinse, dry thoroughly.

To brown blanched almonds : bake as for hazelnuts (above).

To chop almonds : first blanch, skin, chop and then brown them in the oven, if desired.

To shred almonds : first blanch, skin, split in two and cut each half lengthways in fine pieces. These can then be used as they are or browned quickly in the oven, with or without a sprinkling of caster sugar.

To flake almonds : first blanch, skin, and cut horizontally into flakes with a small sharp knife.

To grind almonds : first blanch, skin, chop and pound into a paste (use a pestle and mortar, or a grinder, or the butt end of a rolling pin). Home-prepared ground almonds taste much better than the ready-ground variety.

Pistachios : treat as for almonds, but when blanching add a pinch of bicarbonate of soda to the water to preserve the colour.

Pastry

Flaky pastry
8 oz plain flour
pinch of salt
3 oz butter
3 oz lard
$\frac{1}{4}$ pint ice-cold water (to mix)

Method
Sift the flour with salt into a bowl. Divide the fats into four portions (two of butter, two of lard) ; rub one portion — either lard or butter — into the flour and mix to a firm dough with cold water. The amount of water varies with different flour but an average quantity for 8 oz flour is 4-5 fluid oz (about $\frac{1}{4}$ pint or 8-10 tablespoons) ; the finer the flour the more water it will absorb.

Knead the dough lightly until smooth, then roll out to an oblong. Put a second portion of fat (not the same kind as first portion rubbed in) in small pieces on to two-thirds of the dough. Fold in three, half turn the dough to bring the open edge towards you and roll out again to an oblong. Put on a third portion of fat in pieces, fold dough in three, wrap in a cloth or polythene bag and leave in a cool place for 15 minutes.

Roll out dough again, put on remaining fat in pieces, fold and roll as before. If pastry looks at all streaky, give one more turn and roll again.

Puff pastry
8 oz plain flour
pinch of salt
8 oz butter
1 teaspoon lemon juice
scant $\frac{1}{4}$ pint water (ice cold)

Method
Sift flour and salt into a bowl. Rub in a piece of butter the size of a walnut. Add lemon juice to water, make a well in centre of flour and pour in about two-thirds of the liquid. Mix with a palette, or round-bladed, knife. When the dough is beginning to form, add remaining water.

Turn out the dough on to a marble slab, a laminated-plastic work top, or a board, dusted with flour. Knead dough for 2-3 minutes, then roll out to a square about $\frac{1}{2}$-$\frac{3}{4}$ inch thick.

Beat butter, if necessary, to make it pliable and place in centre of dough. Fold this up over butter to enclose it completely (sides and ends over centre like a parcel). Wrap in a cloth or piece of grease-proof paper and put in the refrigerator for 10-15 minutes.

Flour slab or work top, put on dough, the join facing upwards, and bring rolling pin down on to dough 3-4 times to flatten it slightly.

Now roll out to a rectangle about $\frac{1}{2}$-$\frac{3}{4}$ inch thick. Fold into three, ends to middle, as accurately as possible, if necessary pulling the ends to keep them rectangular. Seal the edges with your hand or rolling pin and turn pastry half round to bring the edge towards you. Roll out again and fold in three (keep a note of the 'turns' given). Set pastry aside in refrigerator for 15 minutes.

Repeat this process twice, giving a total of 6 turns with a 15 minute rest after each two turns. Then leave in the refrigerator until wanted.

Shortcrust pastry

8 oz plain flour
pinch of salt
4-6 oz butter, margarine, lard or
shortening (one of the commer-
cially-prepared fats), or a mixture
of any two
3-4 tablespoons cold water

Method

Sift the flour with a pinch of salt into a mixing bowl. Cut the fat into the flour with a round-bladed knife and, as soon as the pieces are well coated with flour, rub in with the fingertips until the mixture looks like fine breadcrumbs.

Make a well in the centre, add the water (reserving about 1 table-spoon) and mix quickly with a knife. Press together with the fingers, adding the extra water, if necessary, to give a firm dough.

Turn on to a floured board, knead pastry lightly until smooth. Chill in refrigerator (wrapped in grease-proof paper, a polythene bag or foil) for 30 minutes before using.

Rich shortcrust pastry

8 oz plain flour
pinch of salt
6 oz butter
1 rounded dessertspoon caster
sugar (for sweet pastry)
1 egg yolk
2-3 tablespoons cold water

Method

Sift the flour with a pinch of salt into a mixing bowl. Drop in the butter and cut it into the flour until the small pieces are well coated. Then rub them in with the fingertips until the mixture looks like fine breadcrumbs. Stir in the sugar, mix egg yolk with water, tip into the fat and flour and mix quickly with a palette knife to a firm dough.

Turn on to a floured board and knead lightly until smooth. If possible, chill in refrigerator (wrapped in greaseproof paper, a polythene bag or foil) for 30 minutes before using.

To bake blind

Chill pastry case, line with crumpled greaseproof paper and three-parts fill with uncooked rice or beans. An 8-inch diameter flan ring holding a 6-8 oz quantity of pastry should cook for about 26 minutes in an oven at 400°F or Mark 6. Take out paper and beans for last 5 minutes baking.

Poaching fruit

The most important point to remember when cooking fruit is that the water and sugar should first be made into a syrup. An average proportion for this syrup is 3 rounded tablespoons granulated sugar to $\frac{1}{2}$ pint water per lb of fruit. Heat gently in a pan to dissolve sugar, boil rapidly for 2 minutes before the fruit is added. The syrup may be flavoured with pared lemon rind or a vanilla pod.

Prepare fruit as directed in recipe, then place rounded side down in a pan with syrup and bring very slowly to boil. Allow syrup to boil up and over fruit and then reduce heat, cover pan and leave to simmer very gently until tender.

Even fully ripe fruit must be thoroughly cooked to allow the syrup to penetrate, sweeten and prevent discolouration.

Redcurrant jelly

It is not possible to give a specific quantity of redcurrants as the recipe is governed by the amount of juice made, which is variable.

Method

Wash the fruit and, without removing from the stems, put in a 7 lb jam jar or stone crock. Cover and stand in deep pan of hot water. Simmer on top of the stove or in the oven at 350°F or Mark 4, mashing the fruit a little from time to time, until all the juice is extracted (about 1 hour).

Then turn fruit into a jelly bag or double linen strainer, and allow to drain undisturbed overnight over a basin.

Watchpoint To keep the jelly clear and sparkling, do not try to speed up the draining process by forcing juice through ; this will only make the jelly cloudy.

Now measure juice. Allowing 1 lb lump or preserving sugar to each pint of juice, mix juice and sugar together, dissolving over slow heat. When dissolved, bring to the boil, boil hard for 3-5 minutes and skim with a wooden spoon. Test a little on a saucer : allow jelly to cool, tilt saucer and, if jelly is set, it will wrinkle. Put into jam jars place small circles of greaseproof paper over jelly, label and cover with jam pot covers. Store in a dry larder until required.

Rice, boiled

Cook the rice (2 oz washed rice per person) in plenty of boiling, well-salted water (3 quarts per 8 oz rice) for about 12 minutes. You can add a slice of lemon for flavour. Stir with a fork to prevent rice sticking while boiling, and watch that it does not overcook.

To stop rice cooking, either tip it quickly into a colander and drain, or pour $\frac{1}{2}$ cup cold water into the pan and then drain. Pour over a jug of hot water to wash away the remaining starch, making several holes through the rice with the handle of a wooden spoon to help it drain more quickly.

Salad dressings

Boiled dressing
1 tablespoon sugar
1 dessertspoon plain flour
1 teaspoon salt
1 dessertspoon made mustard
1 tablespoon water
$\frac{1}{4}$ pint each vinegar and water (mixed)
1 egg
$\frac{1}{2}$ oz butter
cream, or creamy milk

Method
Mix dry ingredients together, add mustard and about 1 tablespoon water. Add to vinegar and water and cook thoroughly for about 5 minutes. Beat egg, add butter, pour on the hot vinegar mixture and beat thoroughly.

When cold dilute with cream or milk and mix well. This dressing keeps well, covered, in a refrigerator.

French dressing
Mix 1 tablespoon wine, or tarragon, vinegar with $\frac{1}{2}$ teaspoon each of salt and freshly ground black pepper. Add 3 tablespoons of salad oil.

When dressing thickens, taste for correct seasoning ; if it is sharp yet oily, add more salt. Quantities should be in the ratio of 1 part vinegar to 3 parts oil.

For **vinaigrette dressing** add freshly chopped herbs of your choice.

Mayonnaise
2 egg yolks
salt and pepper
dry mustard
$\frac{3}{4}$ cup salad oil
2 tablespoons wine vinegar

This recipe will make $\frac{1}{2}$ pint of mayonnaise.

Method

Work egg yolks and seasonings with a small whisk or wooden spoon in a bowl until thick ; then start adding the oil drop by drop. When 2 tablespoons of oil have been added this mixture will be very thick. Now carefully stir in 1 teaspoon of the vinegar.

The remaining oil can then be added a little more quickly, either 1 tablespoon at a time and beaten thoroughly between each addition until it is absorbed, or in a thin steady stream if you are using an electric beater.

When all the oil has been absorbed, add remaining vinegar to taste, and extra salt and pepper as necessary.

To thin and lighten mayonnaise add a little hot water. For a coating consistency, thin with a little cream or milk.

Eggs should not come straight from the refrigerator. If oil is cloudy or chilled, it can be slightly warmed which will lessen the chances of eggs curdling. Put oil bottle in a pan of hot water for a short time.

Watchpoint Great care must be taken to prevent mayonnaise curdling. Add oil drop by drop at first, and then continue adding it very slowly.

If mayonnaise curdles, start with a fresh yolk in another bowl and work well with seasoning, then add the curdled mixture to it very slowly and carefully. When curdled mixture is completely incorporated, more oil can be added if the mixture is too thin.

Sauces

Basic brown (demi-glace) sauce

3 tablespoons salad oil
1 small onion (finely diced)
1 small carrot (finely diced)
½ stick of celery (finely diced)
1 rounded tablespoon plain flour
1 teaspoon tomato purée
1 tablespoon mushroom peelings (chopped), or 1 mushroom
1 pint well-flavoured brown stock (see opposite)
bouquet garni
salt and pepper

Method

Heat a saucepan, put in the oil and then add diced vegetables (of which there should be no more than 3 tablespoons in all). Lower heat and cook gently until vegetables are on point of changing colour ; an indication of this is when they shrink slightly.

Mix in the flour and brown it slowly, stirring occasionally with a metal spoon and scraping the flour well from the bottom of the pan. When it is a good colour draw pan aside, cool a little, add tomato purée and chopped peelings or mushroom, ¾ pint of cold stock, bouquet garni and seasonings.

Bring to the boil, partially cover pan and cook gently for about 35-40 minutes. Skim off any scum which rises to the surface during this time. Add half the reserved stock, bring again to boil and skim. Simmer for 5 minutes. Add rest of stock, bring to boil and skim again.

Watchpoint Addition of cold stock accelerates rising of scum and so helps to clear the sauce.

Cook for a further 5 minutes, then strain, pressing vegetables gently to extract the juice. Rinse out the pan and return sauce to it. Partially cover and continue to cook gently until syrupy in consistency.

Béchamel sauce

½ pint milk
1 slice of onion
1 small bayleaf
6 peppercorns
1 blade of mace

For roux

¾ oz butter
1 rounded tablespoon plain flour
salt and pepper

Method

Pour milk into a saucepan, add the flavourings, cover pan and infuse on gentle heat for 5-7 minutes. Strain milk and set it aside. Rinse and wipe out the pan and melt the butter in it. To give a white roux remove from heat before stirring in the flour. The roux must be soft and semi-liquid.

Pour on half of milk through a strainer and blend until smooth using a wooden spoon, then add rest of milk. Season lightly, return to a slow to moderate heat and stir until boiling. Boil for no longer than 2 minutes.

Watchpoint If a flour sauce shows signs of lumps, these can be smoothed out by vigorous stirring or beating with a sauce whisk, provided sauce has not boiled ; draw pan aside and stir vigorously. It can then be put back to boil gently for 1-2 minutes before using. If it has boiled and is still lumpy, the only remedy is to strain it.

Sauce madère

1 rounded tablespoon tomato purée
¾ pint demi-glace sauce
½ gill jellied stock (see right)
½ gill Madeira wine
½ oz butter

Method

Add tomato purée to the prepared demi-glace sauce and simmer for 5 minutes, then add stock. Continue to simmer, skimming often, until well reduced. Then add wine and beat in butter. Do not boil after this, but keep warm in a bain-marie or reheat when necessary.

Stocks

Brown bone stock

3 lb beef bones (or mixed beef / veal)
2 onions (quartered)
2 carrots (quartered)
1 stick of celery
large bouquet garni
6 peppercorns
3-4 quarts water
salt

6-quart capacity saucepan, or small fish kettle.

Method

Wipe bones but do not wash unless unavoidable. Put into a very large pan. Set on gentle heat and leave bones to fry gently for 15-20 minutes. Enough fat will come out from the marrow so do not add any to pan unless bones are very dry.

After 10 minutes add the vegetables, having sliced the celery into 3-4 pieces.

When bones and vegetables are just coloured, add herbs, peppercorns and the water, which should come up two-thirds above level of ingredients. Bring slowly to the boil, skimming occasionally, then half cover pan to allow reduction to take place and simmer 4-5 hours, or until stock tastes strong and good.

Strain off and use bones again for a second boiling. Although this second stock will not be so strong as the first, it is good for soups and gravies. Use the first stock for brown sauces, sautés, casseroles, or where a jellied stock is required. For a strong beef broth, add 1 lb shin of beef to the pot halfway through the cooking.

Chicken stock

This should ideally be made from the giblets (neck, gizzard, heart and feet, if available), but never the liver which imparts a bitter flavour. This is better kept for making pâté, or sautéd and used as a savoury. Dry fry the giblets with an onion, washed but not peeled, and cut in half. To dry fry, use a thick pan with a lid, with barely enough fat to cover the bottom. Allow the pan to get very hot before putting in the giblets and onion, cook on full heat until lightly coloured. Remove pan from heat before covering with 2 pints of cold water. Add a large pinch of salt, a few peppercorns and a bouquet garni (bayleaf, thyme, parsley) and simmer gently for 1-2 hours. Alternatively, make the stock when you cook the chicken by putting the giblets in the roasting tin around the chicken with the onion and herbs, and use the measured quantity of water.

Vegetable stock
1 lb carrots
1 lb onions
½ head of celery
½ oz butter
3-4 peppercorns
1 teaspoon tomato purée
1 quart water
salt

Method
Quarter vegetables, brown lightly in the butter in a large pan. Add peppercorns, tomato purée, water and salt. Bring to boil, cover pan and simmer for 2 hours or until the stock has a good flavour.

White bone stock
This stock forms a basis for cream sauces, white stews, etc. It is made in the same way as brown bone stock, except that bones and vegetables are not browned before the water is added and veal bones are used. Do not add the vegetables until the bones have come to the boil and the fat has been skimmed off the liquid.

Bouillon cubes
In an emergency a bouillon cube can be used for certain dishes, but it can never replace properly-made stock because it will lack the characteristic jellied quality. Bouillon cubes are salty and there is always the danger of overdoing the seasoning.

Glossary

Bain-marie (au) To cook at temperature just below boiling point in a bain-marie (a saucepan standing in a larger pan of simmering water). Used in the preparation of sauces, creams and food liable to spoil if cooked over direct heat. May be carried out in oven or on top of stove. A double saucepan gives similar result. Sauces and other delicate dishes may be kept hot in a bain-marie at less than simmering heat.

Bake blind To pre-cook a pastry case before filling (see page 136 for method).

Blanch To whiten meats and remove strong tastes from vegetables by bringing to boil from cold water and draining before further cooking. Green vegetables should be put into boiling water and cooked for up to 1 minute.

Bouquet garni Traditionally a bunch of parsley, thyme, bayleaf, for flavouring stews and sauces. Other herbs can be added. Remove before serving dish.

Butter, clarified Butter from which impurities have been removed by heating gently until foaming, skimming well, straining off clear yellow oil, leaving sediment (milk solids) behind.

Caramelise 1. To dissolve sugar slowly in water, then boil steadily, without stirring, to a coffee-brown colour.
2. To give a thin caramel topping by dusting top of sweet with caster or icing sugar, and grilling slowly.

Deglaze To heat stock and / or wine together with flavoursome sediments left in roasting / frying pan so that gravy / sauce is formed. (Remove excess fat first.)

Flour, seasoned Plain flour to which salt and pepper have been added.

Hull To remove stalks and leaves from strawberries.

Infuse To steep in liquid (not always boiling) in warm place to draw flavour into the liquid.

Julienne strip Strip of vegetable / meat cut to about $\frac{1}{8}$ inch by 1½-2 inches long.

Macerate To soak / infuse, mostly fruit, in liqueur / syrup.

Refresh To pour cold water over previously blanched and drained food. This sets vegetable colours, cleans meat / offal.

Sauté To brown food in butter or oil and butter. Sometimes cooking is completed in a 'small' sauce - ie. one made on the food in the sauté pan.

Scald 1. To plunge into boiling water for easy peeling.
2. To heat a liquid, eg. milk, to just under boiling point.

Slake To mix a flour or other powder with a little cold water before adding to a larger quantity of liquid. This ensures that the powder blends evenly into the liquid, without forming lumps.

Vanilla sugar Sugar delicately flavoured with vanilla (made by storing 1-2 vanilla pods in a jar of sugar).

141

Index

142